Accurate Transit Predictions

Tirupur S. Gopalakrishnan

TRANSLATED BY
SETHUMADHAVAN VENKATRAO

Copyright © Tirupur S. Gopalakrishnan 2024
All Rights Reserved.

ISBN 979-8-89277-981-4

This book has been published with all efforts taken to make the material error-free after the consent of the author. However, the author and the publisher do not assume and hereby disclaim any liability to any party for any loss, damage, or disruption caused by errors or omissions, whether such errors or omissions result from negligence, accident, or any other cause.

While every effort has been made to avoid any mistake or omission, this publication is being sold on the condition and understanding that neither the author nor the publishers or printers would be liable in any manner to any person by reason of any mistake or omission in this publication or for any action taken or omitted to be taken or advice rendered or accepted on the basis of this work. For any defect in printing or binding the publishers will be liable only to replace the defective copy by another copy of this work then available.

Sri Uchista Maha Ganapathaye Namah:

Submitted at the Lotus feet of my Living God

Guruji Tirupur Shri. S. Gopalakrishnan (GK)

Dedication

I offer my humble prayers
To
My Parents
Who have
Parented Me
And
Raised me up
Considering my development
As their own
Bless me Dad
Bless me Mom

PRAYER

Let us submit our prayers to

Our mother

Our Father

Those who were our preceptors and pedagogue till now by touching their lotus feet

Our family deity

Our tutelary God

Our chosen God

Guardian deity

Special/specific deities of the residential town

Let mystics, saints, gurus, spiritual heads, eminent astrologers, the five elements, nature, stellar constellation, the zodiac, the planets, and omnipresent power bless us.

Let our word, actions, and deeds not hurt or hinder people's progress.

Let peace prevail with all.

Sri Uchista Maha Ganapathaye Namah!

Sri Uchista Maha Ganapathaye Namah!

Sri Uchista Maha Ganapathaye Namah!

At the start of every class, I always offer my prayers along the above lines.

I bestow this prayer to everybody.

PRAYERS TO PRECEPTOR

I hereby submit my humble prayers to
my father who is also my first preceptor in astrology

Late **Shri. N. Selvarasu Pillai for** giving me
love, education, pleasure, enlightenment, and knowledge

To my Guru Late Shri. Guru Ramasubbu
To my Guru who leads me in absentia
Late Shri. K. S. Krishnamurthy (K.S.K)

I humbly pray to all saints, spiritual Gurus,
Rishis, and the astrological fraternity.

My greetings to my fellow astrologers.

Seeking the blessings of all
Tirupur S. Gopalakrishnan (Tirupur GK)

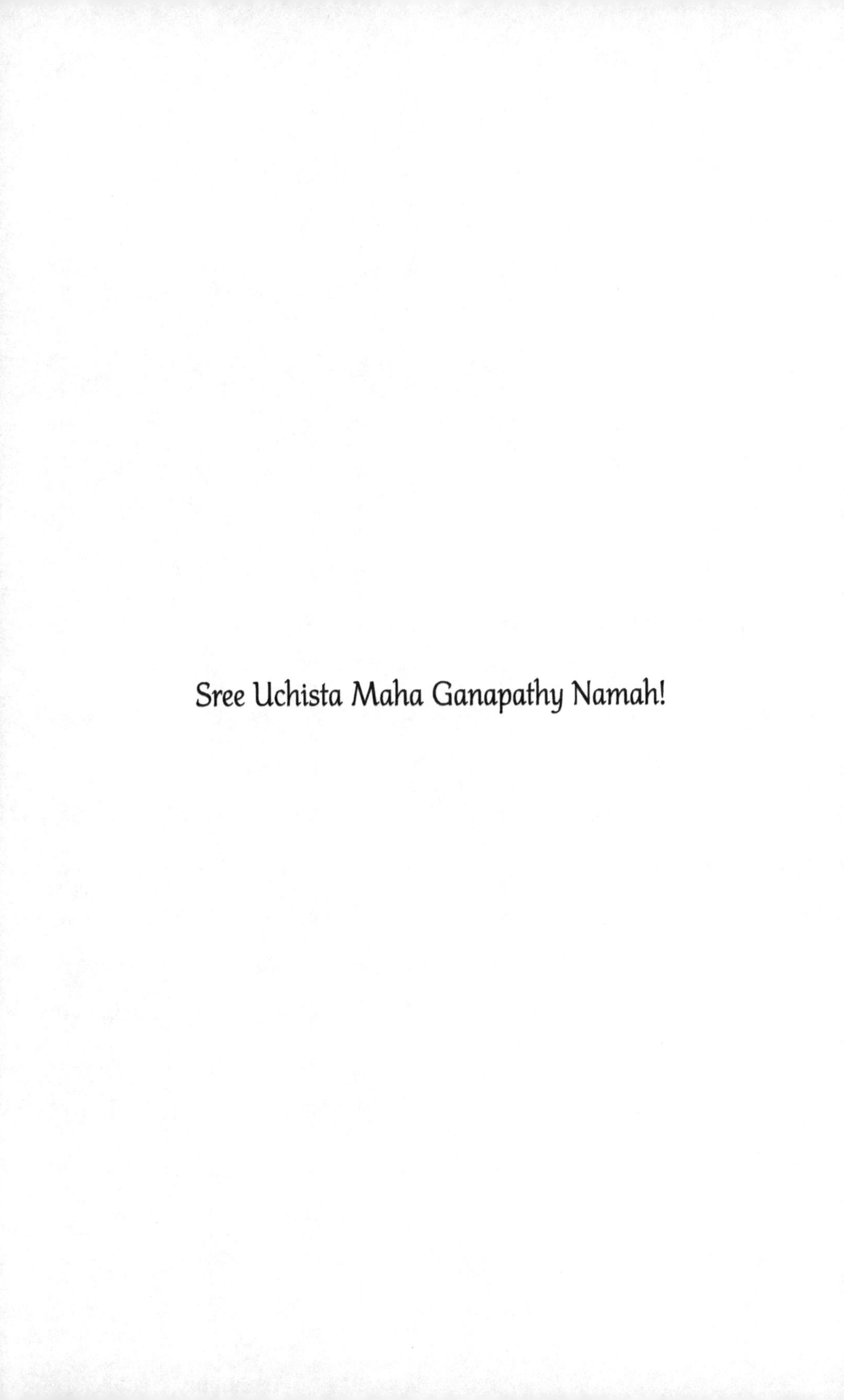

Sree Uchista Maha Ganapathy Namah!

THANKS NOTE

This book was published in Tamil and received attention and appreciation from all.

I humbly thank my mentor and guide of all time Dr. K Nataraj P.hd., (Astro), Oddanchathiram.

I take this opportunity to thank Guruji Shri L. Duraiswamy, Headmaster (Retd) and honorary President of Gurunathar Nadi Astrology Centre.

I would like to thank the Admin of GK Foundation Ms. Aswini K. Thangalakshmi - Sankarankoil for her efforts in the propagation of my astrological thoughts to all through our Foundation.

I also take this opportunity to express my sincere thanks to:

★ Mr. Sankar and MrsTamizharasi Sankar,Tirupur

★ Sri D. Balakrishnan – Axe Oil, Chennai,

★ Sri R. Sakthivel – Ayyappa Label,

★ Sri P. R. Selvaganesh – Bangalore for being the reason for my many books in many languages,

★ My well-wisher Sri Aditya Guruji – Chennai.

★ Mr. Sethumadhavan Venkatrao, Chennai for translating this book into English.

I must also thank

★ Sri S. Suresh – Coimbatore,

★ Sri B. Senthilkumar – Tirupur, all the GK Astro Admin-executives for their tireless support to me.

My sincere thanks to the management, executives, and staff of "Notion Press' for bringing up this book in a fitting manner.

I convey my heartfelt thanks and blessings to everyone.

- Tirupur S. Gopalakrishnan, (Tirupur GK)

9842220903

<u>Gkastro.tirupur@gmail.com</u>

ABOUT THE BOOK. . .

Transit of Planets is not a new phenomenon in Astrology and there are numerous ways to gauge the results of a planetary transit. Of them a few are, a) ascendant-based b) from Moon sign at birth c) from asterism(stars) from where Moon is posited at birth d) from asterism(stars) from where planets are posited e) based on connectivity between planets and finally, f) based on bhavas.

In this book, we are going to see the results in detail about the transit of planets over the planets present in the natal chart. I have reiterated the necessity of correlating the transit with the star, Maha Dasha (Dasha), Antar Dasha (Bukthi), and Prathyantar Dasha (Antharam).

Though many rules were analysed in Nadi principles, here I have penned those which are experienced by me as best in my point of view and successful notions from the tutorials to my students.

Here, results are based on the principles of Sage Parashar, and to explain the results only important planets are shown in the natal chart along with the asterisms in which they are posited in degrees. Planetary conjunctions in Nadi principles and (2, 12, 3, 7, 11) planetary aspects are not considered.

My research concludes that the relativity between the planets discussed and elaborated here in-depth supersede all other methods of transit results. These comments are through the knowledge gained from my preceptors and books read, which are accepted in full or part by me perceived and experienced at length. I firmly believe that my research results will not go wrong, and I take full responsibility if it is confusing or appears wrong in others' perceptions.

Terms such as Sade-Sati, Ashta Sani, and Ashta Guru (Jupiter), are prevalent and are based on the transit of Saturn and Jupiter over the Moon.

Only the results based on the conjunctions and aspects of planets in transit over the natal chart are discussed in this book. The transit of planets over the ascendant, the benefic and inimical aspect of transiting planets, and asterisms based are not taken into account here. Similarly, the transit results based on bhavas are not discussed.

All the above details will run approximately 2400 pages which I have already compiled and scheduled to be released later.

It took me 21 days to complete the writing of this book without any hindrances which is a good omen. Continuous support from friends and other aspects is the success behind the release of this book.

The next part of this book shows more about the transit results and chronicles of the planets.

CONTENTS

1. Various Methods of Transit Results 17

2. Twenty-seven Asterisms 19

3. Transit and Medical Treatment 23

4. Transit = Character, Maha Dasha (Dasha), Antar Dasha (Bukthi) = Events 27

5. Dispositor Theory 29

6. Sun in transit 39

7. Karakathuvas of the Sun 41

8. Moon in Transit 59

9. Karakathuvas of the Moon 61

10. Mars in Transit 69

11. Karakathuvas of Mars 71

12. Role of Mars in Marital relations in Female Horoscopes 73

13. Mercury in Transit 95

14. Karakathuvas of Mercury 97

15. Jupiter in Transit 105

16. The Karakathuvas of Jupiter 107

17. Venus in Transit 129

18. Karakathuvas of Venus 131

19. Saturn in Transit 143

20. Karakathuvas of Saturn 145

21. Rahu in Transit 173

22. Karakathuvas of Rahu 175

23. The Karaka differences between Rahu and Ketu. 191

24. Ketu in Transit. 193

25. Karakathuvas of Ketu. 195

26. Manthi 229

27. Results By Retrograde Planets on Their Return. 235

28. Exchange of Houses 241

29. Exchange of houses leading to the arrest of the fortune of a
    planet due to get or sharing it with the other planet: - 243

30. Combustion 245

31. Dates of Jupiter's Entry into a Rasi/Sign 257

32. Dates of Saturn's Entry into a Rasi/Sign 259

33. Dates of Rahu's Entry into a Rasi/Sign 261

34. Dates of Ketu's Entry into a Rasi/Sign. 263

Back Cover 265

1.

VARIOUS METHODS OF TRANSIT RESULTS

1. Transit effects of a planet under the assumption of its current position as ascendant
2. Transit effects of a planet in relevance to another planet
3. Transit effects of a planet based on its lordship in ascendant-wise considerations
4. Transit effects of a planet based on its current position in a bhava
5. Transit effects of a planet/planets connected to a planet in the natal chart
6. Transit effects by a planet as Maha Dasha (Dasha), Antar Dasha (Bukthi), PrityAntar Dasha Lord
7. Transit effects by a planet as the dispositor of another planet
8. Transit effects by a planet in Jeeva and Sarira considerations
9. Transit effects by a planet as the Sub-lord

The above are some of the methods to arrive at the transit results of planets. However, in this book, we clearly and in detail look at the results of the planetary transit over the planet/planets exhibited in the natal chart.

2.

TWENTY-SEVEN ASTERISMS

(STARS)

1 to 9	9 to 18	19 to 27	Star-Lord	Maha Dasha Period (years)
Aswini	Magha	Moola	Ketu	7
Barani	Poorva-Phalguni	Poorva-Ashada	Venus	20
Krittika	Uttara-Phalguni	Uttara-Ashada	Sun	6
Rohini	Hastha	Shravana	Moon	10
Mrigsira	Chitra	Dhanishta	Mars	7
Arudra	Swathi	Satabhisha	Rahu	18
Punarvasu	Vishaka	Poorva-Bhadra	Jupiter	16
Pushyami	Anuradha	Uttara-Bhadra	Saturn	19
Aslesha	Jyeshta	Revathi	Mercury	17

The above table shows the twenty-seven asterisms (stars) and their respective Dasha lords and Dasha period which should be remembered.

Moon's distancing from 0° to 180° from the Sun is termed a Waxing Moon (Sukla Paksha) gaining strength and moving away from 180° of the Sun is termed a Waning Moon (Krishna Paksha) losing strength. Waxing Moon is considered as benefic while it is considered malefic while waning.

Nine Planets:

Two luminaries the Sun and the Moon. Five planets – Mars, Mercury, Jupiter, Venus, and Saturn. The two nodes termed shadow planets are Rahu and Ketu.

Planetary aspects and control:

9 Planets	Aspect or Control
Ketu	Controls 3, 11 houses
Venus	Aspect 7th house
Sun	Aspect 7th house
Moon	Aspect 7th house
Mars	Aspect 4th, 7th and 8th house
Rahu	Controls 3, 11 houses
Jupiter	Aspect 5th, 7th, and 9th house
Saturn	Aspect 3rd, 7th, and 10th house
Mercury	Aspect 7th house

Pisces (Meena) Exaltation – Venus Debilitation – Mercury Ruler – Jupiter 330° - 360°	Aries (Mesha) Exaltation – Sun Debilitation – Saturn Ruler – Mars 0° - 30°	Taurus (Rishabha) Exaltation – Moon Debilitation – None Ruler – Venus 30° - 60°	Gemini (Mithuna) Exaltation – None Debilitation – None Ruler – Mercury 60° - 90°
Aquarius (Kumbha) Exaltation – None Debilitation – None Ruler – Saturn 300° - 330°	Exaltation Debilitation Ruling Status Of Planets		Cancer (Kataka) Exaltation – Jupiter Debilitation – Mars Ruler – Moon 90° - 120°
Capricorn (Makara) Exaltation – Mars Debilitation – Jupiter Ruler – Saturn 270° - 300°			Leo (Simma) Exaltation – None Debilitation – None Ruler – Sun 120° - 150°
Sagittarius (Dhanus) Exaltation – None Debilitation – None Ruler – Jupiter 240° - 270°	Scorpio (Viruchiga) Exaltation – None Debilitation -Moon Ruler – Mars 210° - 240°	Libra (Thula) Exaltation – Saturn Debilitation – Sun Ruler – Venus 180° - 210°	Virgo (Kanya) Exaltation – Mercury Debilitation – Venus Ruler – Mercury 150° - 180°

A planet debilitates in the 7th house (opposite of) its house of exaltation. Gemini (Mithuna), Leo (Simma), Sagittarius (Dhanus), and Aquarius (Kumbha) find no exalted or debilitated in them. When the question of debilitation or exaltation of the nodes Rahu/ Ketu arises, my answer is negative.

Friendliness and Enmity of Planets:

It is more important to know the Planet's friendlier and envious nature to assess the results during the planetary transit.

Planet	Enemy Planets
Sun	Saturn, Rahu, Ketu
Moon	Rahu, Ketu
Mars	Mercury, Saturn, Rahu, Ketu
Mercury	Moon, Mars, Rahu, Ketu
Jupiter	Rahu, Ketu
Venus	Rahu, Ketu
Saturn	Mars, Rahu, Ketu
Rahu	All Planets
Ketu	All Planets

The above positions of planets are adopted in this book.

3.

TRANSIT AND MEDICAL TREATMENT

Pisces (Meena) Feet Eyes	Aries (Mesha) Head Brain	Taurus (Rishabha) Neck Glands Thyroid Eyes Face	Gemini (Mithuna) Skin Hands Fingers Shoulders
Aquarius (Kumbha) Anklets Blood Breathing	Kalapursha (Time personified) pointers to identify disease		Cancer (Kataka) Respiratory Organs Chest Heart blood circu-lation
Capricorn (Makara) Knee Joints			Leo (Simma) Stomach Heart Large intestine Naval (Umbilical cord)
Sagittarius (Dhanus) Thighs Heart valves Artery	Scorpio (Viruchiga) Uterus Rectum Anus	Libra (Thula) Kidney	Virgo (Kanya) Abdomen Back Spine Smaller intestine Hip

While declaring the disease based on *Kalapurusha* (Time personified), it will be easy to identify the affected part of the body and the extent of affliction.

Operations/Surgeries should not be carried out on the parts of the body denoted by the Rasi/sign over which *the Transit Moon* is passing over. As our body contains more fluids and is the lord of fluids, Moon indicates the nature of the parts of the body.

An astrologer with his exceptional knowledge in asterisms (stars), drekkana (decanates), and sign theories can act as a Doctor/Physician as in the olden days a physician acted as an astrologer and vice versa.

Example:

Stomach/large intestine/naval/umbilical cord-related Surgeries/operations should not be undertaken when the transit Moon is passing over Leo/Simma sign.

Abdomen, uterus, rectum related surgeries/operations should not be carried out while Moon transit over Scorpio/viruchiga Rasi/sign. If surgeries/operations are undertaken the disease will not get cured easily in full and its back effects will remain for a longer period and at times throughout life. Diseases indicated in the parts of the body represented in the *Kalapurusha* (Timer personified) will reflect in the Lagna/ascendant signified parts of the body.

Based on the Planets in the natal chart...

1. The natural character of the native
2. The income sources destined/entitled by the native
3. Lifestyle/circle of the native

Should be ascertained.

Based on the transit Planets...

a) Is there a change in the character/tendencies of the native
b) The present income status/financial sources
c) Is there any radical change at present in the financial conditions of the native

Based on the Maha Dasha (Dasha), Antar Dasha (Bukthi)...

A) What are the events to occur and when?
B) What is the intensity of the event?
C) Whether the native stands to gain or lose due to the event.

The results of the transit will be short-lived and temporary whereas those from the Maha Dasha (Dasha) and Antar Dasha (Bukthi) will be permanent and long-lasting. While the transit indicates ailments of shorter durations, chronic diseases and medicines for a lifetime are indicated by the Maha Dasha (Dasha) and Antar Dasha (Bukthi). To declare the transit results, planetary positions will be more appropriate than bhavagas. Maha Dasha (Dasha) and Antar Dasha (Bukthi) will cause their effects to be based on bhavagas and predictions based on bhavagas will be more precise than that of planetary positions.

4.

TRANSIT = CHARACTER, MAHA DASHA (DASHA), ANTAR DASHA (BUKTHI) = EVENTS

Transit denotes the change or transformation in the Character of a person and temporary events in the life of the native.

E.g. Anger, desires, hatred feelings, and lovemaking not leading to marriage

Maha Dasha (Dasha), and Antar Dasha (Bukthi) describe the permanent events, products/materials/structures, and actions that continue for longer.

While lovemaking that results in marriage is marked by Maha Dasha (Dasha), and Antar Dasha (Bukthi), lovemaking without any desire to marry is indicated by transit.

The birth (natal) chart reflects the thoughts and desires of a native and its implementation is indicated by transit while the Maha Dasha (Dasha) and Antar Dasha (Bukthi) show the currency or fulfilment of the thoughts and desires.

If the planet that induced the desire is posited in the 8th house, it brings disrespect, insult, humiliation, or abasement to the native and on the contrary fame and prosperity when posited in the 9th house.

Jupiter imparts its power to Mars when Mars in the birth (natal) chart receives the aspect of Jupiter in the birth (natal) chart. This power is increased during the transit of Jupiter's aspect to Jupiter in the natal (birth) chart.

Let us assume that Mars is in cancer (Kataka) receiving the 9th aspect of Jupiter in Scorpio (Viruchiga). Jupiter's transit over Pisces (Meena) or Taurus (Rishabha) increases the strength of Mars by its 9th or 7th aspect to natal (birth) Jupiter in Scorpio (Viruchiga).

5.

DISPOSITOR THEORY

A planet will be known as a 'dispositor' when another planet occupies or is posited in its ruling house. For example, if Jupiter is in Aries, then Mars is the dispositer of Jupiter. Let us assume that Mars is the 'dispositor'. If Mars is placed in Capricorn, he will be regarded as a powerful dispositer as Mars gains exalted strength in Capricorn.

If the same Mars is posited in Cancer, he will be considered weak due to his debilitation in Cancer. He will be considered inactive and afflicted in case he is posited with a malefic planet. His affliction in this case as dispositor causes the accident or death of the native.

Dispositor increase or decrease the strength of the planet posited in its ruling house.

The conjunction of benefic and malefic:

In case of a conjunction of a malefic and benefic, the results of both the planets should be declared together. Escalated benefic results and unfavourable malefic results should not be declared.

For example, when Moon and Saturn are combined in Aries, Saturn should not be treated as debilitated as Saturn when associated with Moon gets its debilitation cancelled known as 'neecha banga'. Moon moves faster and Saturn is slow in motion. In case of its conjunction, the native – who has this combination in a birth (natal) chart – if acts faster in his/her actions, will be considered as Moon-centric with a troubled mind.

In case the native is slow in actions, then it can be construed that Saturn powers the native who is a workaholic and very responsible.

Thus, the Karakathuvas of the driving planets should be suitably pinned.

Karakathuvas of Planets and its aspect

Of the 3rd, 7th, and 10th aspects of Saturn over Moon about business, it should be construed that the 7th aspect reveals the wide gap between the thoughts and execution of the business in consideration.

Saturn is the Karaka for business/profession.

When considering Saturn for business/profession…

Saturn should be taken as the business/profession

Rahu causing business hindrances

Ketu creator of crisis in business

Sun is the Commander/Inspection authority/Government representative/Government problems

Moon as the cursor of attention/interest in business/efforts/changes

Mars is the controller/Supervisor

Mercury as the project maintenance/accounts

Jupiter as business improvement/investments/savings

Venus as the venture capital

Mercury associated with **Venus** should be considered as the Bank extending a loan for the business.

Rahu – Ketu as servants under an official.

While considering a planet concerning business, all planets should be correlated with business as under:

Sun – Head/Administrator/Manager

Mars – Security/Supervisor

Saturn – Subordinate of Sun

Rahu-Ketu – Servants of Saturn (As a watchman)

Like-wise everything should be analyzed in terms of business and results should be declared based on that. Such integrations of the planetary karakathuvas enhance the reputation of the Astrologers.

Stellium or Planetary war:

There are different kinds of planetary wars. Prominent among them is the war of transit of malefic planets over the planets in the natal (birth) chart. The native will not enjoy or reap the benefit of the natal (birth) chart planet involved in the planetary war with the transiting planet which may be friendlier or hostile pass over it.

Hostile planets are getting ready for planetary war when they do not receive the aspect of transit Jupiter and running their Maha Dasha (Dasha), Antar Dasha (Bukthi) period.

Result of the Planetary war...

The Planetary war show causes a native by entangling him in a problem that he has not even thought of so far. The intensity of the problem drives the native to take extreme steps in vexation. This is my very best research result. Take a look at it.

Explanation 1

A planet conjunct with a hostile planet in the natal (birth) chart impact when it conjoins another hostile planet during transit exhibiting more vulnerability. When a naturally inimical planet conjoins another inimical planet, it increases their natural enmity gallops resulting in more impact.

Explanation 2

A planet conjoined with a hostile planet in the natal (birth) chart, sheds less impact when conjoins a friendlier planet during transit. The enmity prevalent in the natal (birth) chart changes into friendlier feelings when conjoining a friendlier planet (temporary friendship) in transit.

Explanation 3

A favourable Maha Dasha (Dasha), Antar Dasha (Bukthi) empowers the native to tolerate the fatalities of unfavourable transit of planets. On the contrary, if the Maha Dasha (Dasha), and Antar Dasha (Bukthi) are **also not favourable**, the native has to suffer to an unbearable extent.

Explanation 4

When too many planets are conjoined in the natal (birth) chart, each planet reflects the character of its associated planets during transit. Only when a planet is alone in the sign, it reveals its character and effects in full.

Explanation 5

A planet that has another planet in the same degree of its occupation in another Rasi/sign extends the Karakathuva results of the other planet along with its results during its transit, Maha Dasha (Dasha), Antar Dasha (Bukthi).

Explanation 6

When a transiting planet finds no other planets in the Rasi/sign of its transit, do not confer any major effects or impact to the native.

It is like a guest looking at the locked house of his host.

Explanation 7

If a transiting planet finds a friend in its house of transit, the planet extends good results to the native.

It is something like a guest finds an intimate in the house of his host.

Explanation 8

If a transiting planet finds its enemy in its house of transit, the planet extends the worst results to the native.

It is like a guest facing somebody whom he does not like in the house of his host.

Explanation 9

When a planet finds several planets during its transit entry into a Rasi/sign, necessarily it is compelled to extend the benefits of all the planets and does so in the order of the degree-wise placement of the planets it comes across.

For example, there are three planets in the sequential order of Mars, Rahu, and Jupiter posited in Leo (Simma) natal (birth) chart. Transit Saturn is passing over Leo (simma). Now, Saturn will exert its combined results in the order of its association with Mars as first, with Rahu as Second, and finally with that Jupiter.

Here, Saturn bestows evil effects until crossing a hostile planet and good results while crossing a benefic planet. In transit, Saturn surpasses two evil planets and one benefic /good planet thus extending two-thirds of evil results and one-third of beneficial results.

For Capricorn Rasi/Sign, Saturn's transit in 8th house Leo is termed as 'Ashta Shani' causing evil effects. But it will not impact equally 'Uthra-bhadra' and 'Dhanishta' asterisms and vary depending upon other planets.

Transit of Sun over natal (birth) Saturn

Sun is passing over Leo, its own house in transit where his rival natal (birth) Saturn is posited.

Here, Sun is depicted as a Superior/Manager and Saturn as a sub-ordinate/servant. Sun will extract work from Saturn and will boss over it. Hence, it will be correct to say that the native will face problems from Superiors/Managers/Administrators.

Saturn can be termed as disease and Sun as medicine. As medicine cures the disease, the Sun's transit over Saturn may be construed as relief from the disease caused by the Karaka/bhava of Saturn.

While Saturn is dark, the Sun is compared to light/brightness. It can be assumed that the native's dark life will brighten during the transit of Sun in Leo over natal (birth) Saturn.

The Sun and Saturn as father and son reveal the relationship between them at the time of the transit.

The Sun represents the father/administrator/order while Saturn indicates the son's relationship/son's actions. The father's administrative interruptions will and orders will bother the son who will hate to adopt/obey.

The Sun denotes administration/management and Saturn denotes employee/servant. The native will often face problems and hindrances from the administration/management quite often.

The Sun represents aathma/life and Saturn indicates longevity as their Karakathuvas. Danger to life is caused during the transit of Saturn over the Sun.

The Karakathuvas of both Saturn and the Sun should be combined in astrological predictions.

The results will not be the same during the transit of two planets over the other. The results vary according to who is on the natal planet (birth chart) and who is in transit.

The results are based on friendship, enmity, karakathuvas, and bhava as well.

Let us now see two transits.

The Sun's transit over natal (birth) chart Saturn.

Saturn's transit over the natal (birth) chart Sun.

Saturn's transit over the natal (birth) chart Sun...

The results should be arrived at by linking the Karakathuvas of the Sun to the Karakathuvas of Saturn.

1. The Sun denotes immunity in the body and Saturn denotes disease.
   Result: Saturn decreases immunity and increases the impact of the disease.

2. The Sun denotes Sperm and Saturn denotes deficiency.
   Result: Deficient cells/sperm

3. The Sun denotes the father and Saturn denotes bitterness.
   Result: Bitter/stressed relationship between the father and son. It also indicates bitter paternal relations.

4. The Sun represents administration and Saturn indicates complaints/errors/mistakes.
   Result: The native will find fault with management/administration.

5. The Sun is compared to the Manager/Supervisor and Saturn to the servant/subordinate.
   Result: When the servant/subordinate works more than the Manager/Supervisor or does the work of the Manager/Supervisor, then he will not respect his superiors or obey their orders. Here, the positions of the planet should be noted thoroughly.

6. A clear distinction between the natal and transit of who is where should be noted before giving the results.

7. As Saturn decimates/removes the security given by the Karakathuva/bhava of the Sun, the parts denoted/conserved by the Sun will be affected.

8. The Sun is responsible for contagious/infectious diseases. Human waste like excreta and urine are the karakathuvas of Saturn. This transit exposes the infection through human waste like urine and human excreta.

9. The Sun represents life and Saturn the longevity as their respective karakathuvas.
   The transit reforms life or lessens longevity depending upon the nature of the planet involved.

10. The Sun is the Kharaga for the soul while the subconsciousness is the Kharaga of Saturn. This transit enables transcendental meditation to energize the soul. A keen observation of the planets will help us to mark their reactions.

We should distinguish the natal and transit planets before arriving at the results.

Results due to the conjunction of the Sun + Saturn:

1. There will be differences of opinion between the father and the son resulting in a lack of unity in the family
2. There will be differences of opinion between the Manager and subordinates/workers
3. There will be bitterness between the co-parceners/co-born concerning ancestral properties.
4. There will be a deficiency in blood cells.

Planets in the natal (birth) chart point to the above happenings to the native.

Transit:

The above results can be experienced during the **transit** of the Sun or Saturn over the sign in which this planetary combination (Sun + Saturn) is present. This may happen even when their malice planets transit over the Sun or Saturn.

Rule 1

The transit Sun should either be in Taurus or Scorpio. Saturn should be posited in Taurus, Leo, Scorpio, or Pisces. This indicates that the transiting Sun and Saturn should connect with the Sun + Saturn combination.

Rule 2

Inimical planets to the Sun or Saturn should be transiting through Taurus. The level of impact depends upon the current Maha Dasha (Dasha), and Antar Dasha (Bukthi). This impact may be felt either during a) Sun Maha Dasha (Dasha) and Saturn Antar Dasha (Bukthi) or b) Saturn Maha Dasha (Dasha). Else it may be Saturn Antar Dasha (bukthi) of the Maha Dasha (Dasha) of inimical planets to Saturn.

Every planet assumes the qualities and transit planets posited in the trines to asterisms in which it is positioned. This helps in future predictions.

When more than one planet is involved in transit, the results are based on combined planetary effects.

What is the difference between the transit of individual planets and that of combined planetary transit?

While the transit of individual planets affects only the native, combined planetary transit affects the entire family of the native.

6.

SUN IN TRANSIT

Surya Gayathri:

Ohm Asvathvajaaya vidhmahe

Paasa hasthaya deemahi

Thanno Surya prachodayath

Let Lord Surya bestow his blessings on us to understand all his Karaka, bhava, and transit results

Transit Results:

When transit Sun Passover his friendlier planets, the karaka of Sun will become meritorious and weaken while moving over his rivals.

7.

KARAKATHUVAS OF THE SUN

General nature of the Sun: –

Prestige, trust, integrity, soul, management, administration, daytime, not so destructive but essential fire, anger, warrior (Kshatriya), lord of the daytime.

Karaka for dreams and imagination. A native dreams too big about his life when he has the Sun posited in the 3rd, 7th, or 11th house. The Sun posited in the 7th induces extraordinary dreams to the extent of playing spoil fort in the domestic life of the native rather than its placement in the 3rd or 11th houses.

The Sun denotes the social status and managerial capacity of an individual. The Sun in fire Signs Aries, Leo, and Sagittarius increases body temperature resulting in bile diseases. In watery signs Cancer, Scorpio, and Pisces affects progeny.

The Sun in relations/persons: –

The Sun designated the father, status of the father, eldest son, father-in-law after marriage, and spiritual heads.

The Sun as parts of the body/disease: –

The right eye, body temperature, migraine, short sight, long sight, throat and heat-related diseases, paranoia or mental disorder, bile diseases, spine, backbone, and big toe are pointed by the Sun.

The Sun in places: –

Hilly regions, elevated places, multi-story buildings, forests, forts, lodges, apartments and group houses, buildings that fetch fixed income, rental resources, commercial complexes, terraces, and shed are some places represented by the Sun.

The Sun in Government relations: -

Government, politics, administrator, lender, and borrower on the Government side, power, leadership responsibilities, augmenters of Government revenue, decisions of the Government to deduce crime or punishment, village or town heads.

The Sun's representation as God and in worship: -

Soul worship, worship of light-based forms, worship of Lord Shiva, Shiv Rupa, Shiv lingam, Shiv stotras, names of Shiva.

Articles/products represented by the Sun: -

Round/circular shaped Golden-ornaments, Aaras (arc-shaped jewels), thick trees.

Occupations indicated by the Sun: -

If the Sun happens to be the indicator of occupation in a natal (birth) chart, he gives one of the below as the occupation of the native:

A Government job, Manager/administrator, jewellery business, gold plating/polishing, local government establishments, taluk, municipalities, power establishments, judge, people representatives as M.L.A, M.P. in the Government, Doctors, inflammable and gas, hereditary business.

Transit results:

When amicable or benefic planets of the Sun transit over the natal (birth) chart Sun it confers auspicious/good results and extends inauspicious/bad results while his enemy planets transit over the natal (birth) chart Sun.

Transit Sun...

Daily the Sun moves 00 degrees, 58 minutes, 08 seconds. The Sun takes 03 days, 22 hours, and 55 minutes to pass over one part of an asterism (star) and approximately one day to cross one degree. It takes one month to cross each sign and takes a year to go around the zodiac.

During the currency of Maha Dasha (Dasha), Antar Dasha (Bukthi), and PrithyAntar Dasha (Anthra) of the Sun, his transit extends extensive good or bad results. It will be less when the Sun Maha Dasha (Dasha), Antar Dasha (Bukthi), and PrithyAntar Dasha (Anthra) are not in operation. The Sun in transit confers minimum benefits.

When another planet is conjoined to the natal (birth) chart Sun, a transiting planet approaching the Sun will give varied results. Similarly, the planet which is posited in the Sun's asterism (Krittiga, Uthra-Phalguna, Uthra-ashada) will possess the Karakathuva of the Sun during its transit. These differences should be borne in mind as the Sun is the deciding authority of the month for the event to occur in all the events.

During the transit of the Sun, the planets posited in the Sun's house (Leo) and asterisms (Krittiga, Uthra-Phalguna, and Uthra-ashada) slightly alter the results extended by the Sun.

The Sun is a monthly planet, that keeps changing the results given to the native every month. The results of the Sun's transit can be experienced when a planet is posited in the sign of transit.

Results of the Sun's transit over natal (birth) chart Sun: -

This transit energizes the body. The results related to the bhava to which the Sun becomes the Lord can be harvested. The aspect of other planets over the Sun varies the results. There will be changes in the results if the Sun is exalted in the natal (birth) chart while he transits in his sign of debilitation.

Example:

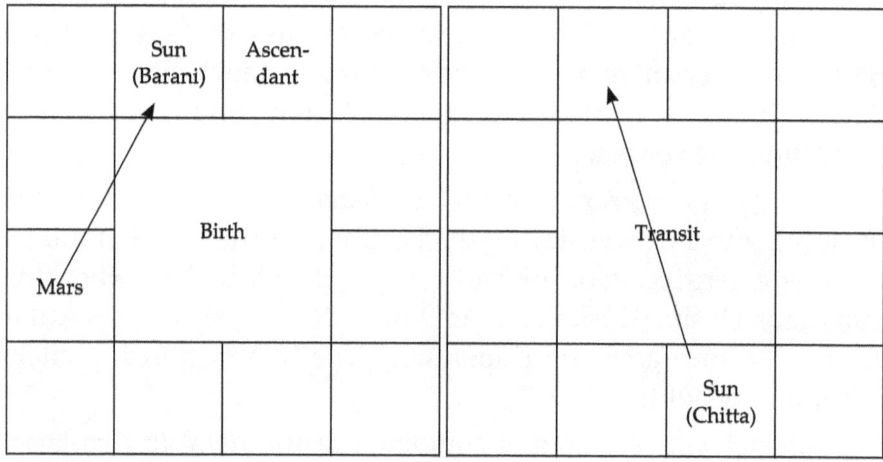

In the above chart, the Sun is exalted in Aries. Mars in Capricorn aspects the Sun in the Aries through its 4th aspect. Each year the Sun will pass its debilitation point in Libra once. Hence this native will face problems, mental torture/depression, and loss as the Sun portrays as the lord of the 4th bhava Leo from Taurus ascendant. At the same time, the Sun denotes infectious diseases. Had the native suffered from infectious diseases, the intensity of the disease will decrease during the transit of the Sun in Libra. As the 4th aspect of Mars falls on the (natal) Sun in Aries and the Sun's transit in Chitta (Chithirai) - the asterisms of Mars in Libra, these results will be experienced by the native.

As the Sun represents the 4th bhava lord and the father as his Karakathuva, the impact will be on the mother in domestic management and the father in the family's economic support.

Transit of the Sun over the Moon in the natal (birth) chart: -

Unafflicted Moon's status shows a stable/undisturbed position of the native/his mother. Mother's management capacities will increase bringing disgrace to the father. At the same time, imaginations and worries will haunt the mother of the native due to her interventions in family management. Skin diseases will affect.

Afflicted Moon causes depression in the native/his mother.

Transit of the Sun over Mars in the natal (birth) chart: -

1. Elders in despair with the native will visit him
2. The Expected loan against the house property will fructify but the amount will be less. The native will not lose the property.
3. Elder siblings will get recognition, prestige, and a good name. Higher officials will be friendlier.
4. For those with loans against their house properties, the loaner will visit and value the house. In case of a good valuation, the loanee will lose the property.
5. It will be hard times for those who have invested in products that could be affected by thunder and lighting.
6. For those who are engaged in engineering industries, skilled managers will approach and support earnings through machinery. New projects will be received.
7. The temperature of the blood in the body will hot up causing disease. Blood-related diseases will crop up. Headache and heartbeat-related diseases will bother the native. Ladies will face menstruation problems.

Example:

Ascendant							
	Birth				Transit		
			Mars (Purva-phalguna)				Sun
			Venus				

For Pisces ascendant, Mars is posited in Leo, the house of the Sun in the Purva-Phalguna asterism belonging to Venus. The transit Sun passes over natal (birth) Mars. The body temperature of the natives hot up and suffered from heat-related diseases.

As one hot planet is passing over another hot planet, the body temperature increases. As Mars is posited in the 6th house of Pisces ascendant, it has become a disease.

The Sun being a monthly planet, once a year will travel over Mars raising a question as to the return of disease each year.

The Sin in transit transforms any one of the multiple Karakathuvas that Mars possesses based on the results of Maha Dasha (Dasha) and Antar Dasha (Bukthi). This transit should be correlated to the age of the native.

When the results are computed for a female, it should be reckoned that an elderly person will visit the female's family to talk about her marriage-related events.

As Mars represents the husband in a female natal (birth) chart, the results should be based on that. As Mars is posited in Purva-Phalguna, an asterism belonging to Venus and its position in 7th Bhava, it may either a) an elderly person will visit the girl's family to discuss marriage-related issues or a manager/administrator will visit to talk about money-related issues as the Sun represents Management and Mars represents machinery.

Example: -

<table>
<tr><td>Ascen-
dant</td><td></td><td></td><td></td><td></td><td></td><td></td><td></td></tr>
<tr><td>Ketu 15°</td><td rowspan="2">Birth</td><td></td><td></td><td rowspan="2">Transit</td><td></td></tr>
<tr><td></td><td>Mars 10°
Rahu 15°</td><td></td><td>Sun 8°</td></tr>
<tr><td></td><td></td><td></td><td></td><td></td><td></td><td></td><td></td></tr>
</table>

In the case of female horoscopes (natal charts): -

For Pisces ascendant, Mars is posited in the grip of Rahu in the Sun's house Leo and the transit Sun is passing over it. As Mars is posited in the 6th house to Pisces, it denotes the problems leading to the separation of husband and wife.

Here the Sun represents his father-in-law and he visits his daughter's house to advise his son-in-law who is deficient in character.

The father-in-law speaks to his daughter's husband and gets humiliated as here Rahu represents humiliation (The Sun is closing in on Rahu's position). Hence a detailed degree-wise analysis will throw enhanced results.

This can also be in the following lines: -

a) Before marriage, in the female chart, the Sun denotes the father of the girl and Mars as her brother. So here it should be construed that the father discusses about his daughter with her brother. After marriage, the Sun represents the father-in-law as Mars becomes his daughter's husband, thereby depicting the dialogue between the father-in-law and his daughter's husband. Hence while casting the results, age, time, and Karaka relationship should be reckoned.

b) Mars + Rahu combination defines the problem relating to the house and landed property while the Sun defines the village head and other elders, father or father-in-law. This indicates the dispute in house and landed property concerning the female and the father's visit to her house accompanied by the village head and other elderly people to discuss.

Transit of the Sun over Mercury in the natal (birth) chart: -

Students will be induced to brisk learning. Elders will interfere in love affairs. If the love affair blossom in an office environment, the employer/manager/administrator/supervisor will interrupt and cause damages. In a school environment, the management will intrude on all affairs. In a family, the father will gain through land dealings.

Many people will get clear wisdom and understand who and what they are. Mercury posited in low degrees will cause diseases related to Karakathuvas of Mercury which are skin, veins, mental aberration, etc.,

Those who are running educational institutions like schools and colleges will get good executives like Principals and administrators. The Correspondent will inspect the institution.

Senior Bank officials, authorities, and executives will inspect the Bank and loan sanctioning authorities/officials. Here Bank employees are represented by Mercury and Bank Managers/ inspecting authorities by the Sun.

It will be good to worship the Lords of Shiva and Vishnu in a combined form of Lord Shankara Narayana as Mercury depicts Lord Vishnu and the Sun to Lord Shiva.

The transit of the Sun over natal (birth) Mercury can also be understood as:

Fencing a vacant lord to secure it. Pillar wire fencing will be indicated by the combination of the Sun + Rahu/Ketu and Compound wall fencing will be indicated by Sun + Mars combination. Employing one for security is indicated by the combination of the Sun, Mars, and Saturn as the Sun describes the Senior Security Officer, Mars as the security officer, and security by the Mars + Saturn combination.

The transit of the Sun over natal (birth) chart Jupiter: -

This reveals the monthly traveller of soul indicator Sun over the yearly devotion indicator Jupiter. This period refers to the adoption of a spiritual, devotion path by the native.

As the Sun and Jupiter are lords of the trines and friendlier between them, there will be no worst change in the character of the native, and whatever change happens will be on good terms. But more harm can be felt in bhava results.

This transit will chasten the native (Him/Her).

There will be a deficient sperm count in the case of male natives. Drugs used to improvise sperm count will increase body temperature compelling the native to seek alternative medicine. Jupiter denotes sperm cells and heat by the Sun.

This transit affects those who have liver, intestine, brain, and bone disorders. Those with Jupiter in the lowest or Highest degrees in their natal (birth) chart should fear diseases/disorders.

The natives might be compelled to lose ancestral properties to keep their prestige intact. They will also involve in public activities to keep their respect and earn spiritual merits.

This transit will cause worries about progeny for those who are childless, their social status, and their self-esteem.

Example:

	Father				Sun (Pur-va-Bhadra)		
Jupiter 3° Sun 1°	Birth				Transit		
		Ascen-dant					

The above native has Jupiter posited at 3.52° and the Sun at 1.23°. As both are posited in very low degrees in their sign, during their transit,

1. The native's father suffered from jaundice and died after severe suffering. (Jupiter is the karaka for jaundice).
2. The native had cancer in his neck and survived after surgery.

The Sun's placement in Aquarius – the bhadagasthana 'house of evil' 11th house of Aries, which represents the 9th house (an indicator of father) from the Leo ascendant is the important reason for the death of the native's father and native's survival. As Jupiter is the lord of the evil 8th house for Leo's ascendant conjoined the Sun, the transit and Maha Dasha (Dasha), and Antar Dasha (Bukthi) connecting the Sun and Jupiter play a vital role in the results.

Note: –

A planet posited in the lowest degree is considered to be very weak while one in the highest degree is very strong. Both extend their results in different proportions. Once they infect through disease, it will be very difficult to cure.

Example: - 2

<table>
<tr><td></td><td>Sun 1°
Jupiter 3°</td><td></td><td></td></tr>
<tr><td rowspan="2"></td><td colspan="2" rowspan="2">Birth</td><td rowspan="2"></td></tr>
<tr></tr>
<tr><td></td><td></td><td></td><td></td></tr>
</table>

<table>
<tr><td></td><td>Sun 9°</td><td></td><td></td></tr>
<tr><td rowspan="2"></td><td colspan="2" rowspan="2">Transit</td><td rowspan="2"></td></tr>
<tr><td>Jupiter
15°
(Sravana)</td></tr>
<tr><td></td><td></td><td></td><td></td></tr>
</table>

The native has Jupiter at 3.10° and the Sun at 1.50°. Thoughts about lack of progeny, social respect, and social status bothered the native throughout this transit.

During the transit of the Sun over the natal (birth) chart Jupiter, it constituted the travel of the Sun in the 'Vedhai' (star of affliction) star of the transiting Jupiter. The native was taking medical treatment for progeny. The effect of drugs caused serious side effects.

The thoughts about remaining childless bothered the natives much during the transit of the Sun over natal (birth) chart Jupiter rather than other periods. He denoted heavily for temple renovation during this period.

The transit of the Sun over natal (birth) Venus: -

This transit causes wasteful expenditures of money due to the travel of planet of heat over the planet representing money. As both are monthly planets, the results will be faster and fade away quickly. The concern should be about the Maha Dasha (Dasha), Antar Dasha (Bukthi), and PrithyAntar Dasha (Anthram) of both the planets and their respective bhavas, as it will produce good results.

The Father/father-in-law will be interested in money during this period and focus on scrutiny of money transactions and any mistakes in it will push him into trouble for a month.

The father will be fond of luxurious items and indulge in lavish expenses. When his expenses are condemned or curtailed unnecessary problems will crop up.

If in a company, the manager or administrator will be intimate with other women which may be marital relations ending in a problematic marriage.

Diseases concerned with the eyes and glands in the body will be stimulated during this transit. This should be feared only if Venus is in the lowest or highest degrees in the sign where it is posited.

The native will be inclined towards sexual pleasure due to increased body temperature.

Medical treatment towards hormones during this transit results in abnormal disease. Artificial fertilities and doubtful medical treatments suggested by doctors should not be attempted. Other doubtful forms of medical treatment and medicines should not be adhered to. For serious diseases, poison-coated medicines give successful results. (Sources reveal that snake poison cures Cancer.)

Transit of the Sun over natal (birth) Saturn: -

This is the transit of a luminary over a dark planet. The travel of a soul representative over the yearly karmic planet. The karma-related activities should be carefully executed else mistakes will be immediately indicated. As this is the transit of a monthly planet over a yearly planet, the results will change in a very short period. It should be checked to see whether the Maha Dasha (Dasha), Antar Dasha (Bukthi), and Prithyanthat Dasha (Anthram) of the transiting planets are in operation and also the bhavagas relating to which is in operation.

1. The health of the father will deteriorate. Had his health or that of the elders in the family is already in an affected stage,

they will be facing serious near-death conditions and even death depending upon their bad Maha Dasha (Dasha), Antar Dasha (Bukthi), and Prithy Antar Dasha (Anthram).

2. Executives could not extract work from their subordinates/ servants. At the same time, their superiors will be harsh on them and servants/subordinates/employees will be squeezed.

3. When this transit is experienced in the 7th bhava, the marriage will sour due to imagination, dreams, and impractical thoughts.

4. Treatments for progeny will be successful as the sperm count will increase.

5. Hard and sincere workers will win accolades and be respected by superiors.

6. There will be interference and interruptions from the superiors in the native's work/job/profession and has to protest to get recognition in service.

7. As this transit is between two different significators, the native may lose faith in himself.

8. The transit of the Sun will not hinder the natives much if Saturn is conjoined by Venus, and Jupiter as they will protect the botheration to Saturn by the Sun. The Sun's travel over Saturn associated with Venus will reduce the impact of the troubles extended by the father to the native (Sun father, Saturn – son) in the form of a sister or aunt. (Venus – sister/ aunt). The monetary transactions between the father and son will resolve the problems in their absence.

Example: –

		Ascendant					
	Birth				Transit		
		Saturn 28°					Sun

In relation, the Sun indicates the father and Saturn as his son.

The father of the above native helped his son to establish a business. During the transit of the Sun over Saturn, the father was very stringent/strict with his son who took it as humiliation and has to remain in exile. The father condemned his son as useless and want him not even fit to stand before his corpse. All this happened over a period of just 30 days.

Each year son considered this period a lethal scenario, as the Sun passes over Saturn once a year.

Both the father and the son grieved about each other.

The same planetary condition prevailed in a female horoscope (natal chart). The girl's father supported his daughter who confronted her husband and, after behaving harshly with his son-in-law, brought her home. His daughter who was submissive and justified her father's advice and action during the transit of the Sun over natal (birth) Saturn, turned hostile after the Sun crossed Saturn. She felt for her father's action. The transit changes the course of action in an event.

Example: -

<table>
<tr><td></td><td></td><td></td><td></td><td></td><td></td><td></td></tr>
<tr><td>Ketu</td><td rowspan="2">Birth</td><td></td><td></td><td rowspan="2">Transit</td><td></td></tr>
<tr><td></td><td>Saturn
Rahu</td><td></td><td>Sun</td></tr>
<tr><td></td><td></td><td></td><td></td><td></td><td></td></tr>
</table>

Transit Sun is passing over his sign Leo where Saturn and Rahu are posited in the natal (birth) chart.

Here Saturn shall be compared to the servant and the Sun to the executive/administrator. Saturn conjoined and induced by Rahu overpowers the Sun who suffers in the collision. The native with due justification for his actions or by exercising power refuses to obey his administrator/superiors, forcing them to bow down. The native will cause loss of job/profession to his superiors/administrators by involving them in a corruption case by offering them bribes. (Rahu is responsible/indicator of bribe/corruption).

In this case, had Saturn been alone in Leo, the Sun will dictate and made Saturn obey by bringing it under his control. Rahu conjoined with Saturn reverses the actions.

(It should be imagined like Saturn, though rented the house owned by the Sun, residing with Rahu, a foe of the Sun, joining hands to oppose the Sun).

Transit of the Sun over natal (birth) Rahu: -

This refers to the transit of a monthly planet over a yearly planet indicating the collision of inimical planets which will impact the native in the worst way. This will impart bad temperament **compulsorily** on the Karaka relations indicated by the Sun.

During the Sun's transit period of one month, any one of the fathers/fathers-in-law/ elderly persons will be subjected to bad company **voluntarily** which will be hard to revive.

Those in Government service will be lured by excessive money making and getting caught by law enforcing authorities as the Sun indicates Government and Rahu in corrupt actions.

It also indicates the family head's sufferings by borrowing heavily at a higher rate of interest for family maintenance.

This transit also indicates the inability to pay interest from earnings and non-redeemable pledged articles but forcing the native to indulge in such borrowing actions. Instead of moving away from such problematic situations, the native will be drawn toward them.

This transit may induce expectations of undue respect, which may turn out to be false prestige, and irrelevant to the native.

The native could not get a chance to take the right and proper decision during this transit. People in higher positions slide by taking wrong decisions during this transit.

Keeping faith in luck, the native may try to augment his income during this transit and receive a little favour.

Transit of the Sun over natal (birth) Ketu: -

This refers to the transit of a monthly planet over a yearly planet indicating the collision of inimical planets which will impact the native in the worst way. This will impart or try to impart spiritual path compulsorily on the Karaka relations indicated by the Sun.

Any one of the members of the family - the father or father-in-law or an elderly person or the son will turn towards a spiritual path during this transit.

Some will engage themselves in 'Satsang' (seeking the good through spiritual dialogues) activities and do service in the temple and spiritual societies while some may undertake a pilgrimage to holy places. Some atheists will do communal, political party services. Activities during this transit will receive special mention.

This transit also indicates Government Punishment as the Sun marks the Government and Ketu to legal actions and punishment.

Who is affected by this transit?

1. Those who have Rahu/Ketu conjoined with the Sun in their natal (birth) chart.
2. Those who have Rahu/Ketu posited in trines to the sign where the Sun is.
3. Those who have their Rahu/Ketu posited in the asterisms of the Sun or the Sun posited in the asterisms of Rahu/Ketu.
4. Those who have their Sun and Rahu/Ketu in the same degrees or both the Sun and Rahu/Ketu posited in the same part of asterism position (Both in part 1 or part 2, etc.,)
5. Those who are running either Sun Maha Dasha (Dasha) and Antar Dasha (Bukthi) or Rahu/Ketu Maha Dasha (Dasha) and Sun Antar Dasha (Bukthi).

8.

MOON IN TRANSIT

Lord Chandra (Moon) Gayathri:

Ohm Padmathvajaya vidhmahe

Hema rupaya deemahi

Thanno Somah prachodayath

Let Lord Chandra (Moon) bestow his blessings on us to understand all his

Karaka, bhava, and transit results

Transit Results: -

The transit of the Moon over its friendlier planets the Karaka relations of the Moon will be meritorious and will be impacted while moving over inimical planets.

9.

KARAKATHUVAS OF THE MOON

The general disposition of the Moon: -

Temptations, mind, devaluation/depreciation, changes, all secret/ mischievous/stealthy activities, thief, notoriety, actions that result in humiliation, freebies, memory and memory loss, suspicion, danger in the water, pleasures enjoyable through mind and body. As the moon is an indicator of travel, the karaka relations pointed by the planet over which the Moon passes over will undertake a journey or the native will travel on behalf of that Karaka relation.

Relation/persons indicated by the Moon: -

Mothers, Mother-in-law after marriage, old aged ladies, the general public, people engaged in public service (salesmen, conductors, etc.,), employees in public work departments, distributors of freebies, those who utter the words 'often', poets when Moon is not afflicted, story writers, imaginative characters, psychotic patients when Moon is afflicted.

Parts of the body/diseases indicated by the Moon: -

Body, mind, blood circulation, breastfeeding, left eye, feelings, uterus in case of ladies, menstruation problems, chest, wisdom/ wit, fluids in the body, cold.

Places denoted by the Moon: -

Water bodies, milk storage, lactating trees, dining hall, pearl, lockers containing pearl ornaments, bedroom, travel robes.

God/worship referred by the Moon: -

Goddess (Ambal), Goddess without adornment, and family (tutelary) gods.

Products represented by the Moon: -

Milk-like liquids and juices, Milk, lactating trees, pearl ornaments.

Business products indicated by the Moon: -

Businesses in daily perishables like food, flower, coconut, paddy, rice, provision stores, cotton, milk, juices, and cool drinks, vegetable vendors, fruits stalls, hotels, restaurants, food products, water, and water-related businesses, black magic, sailors, liquor, washermen/dhobi, advertisement, eatables, milk products, curd, butter, traders, seafaring activities, fish and dry fish, sea foods, salt, fertilizers, agriculture, products from the sea like oysters, pearls, etc.,

Moon in marital relations: -

The Moon defines body and mind as its karaka qualities. An unspoiled moon keeps the mind intact.

The moon when conjoins malefic planets or her inimical planets will mar the mind and damage the family life.

In fiery houses the Moon points and administrative capabilities, patience in earthly signs, mental turbulence in windy/air signs, and sentimental feelings in watery signs.

Transit Moon: -

The Moon takes one and a half an hour to one hour forty-five minutes to pass over 1° and 6 hours to cross 1 part of a star. To fully pass over a sign Moon takes fifty-four hours and 27 days to complete one cycle of the zodiac.

If the native is running Moon Maha Dasha (Dasha), Antar Dasha (Bukthi), or PrithyAntar Dasha (Anthram) during the transit Moon, he will reap good or bad results in excess and the good or bad results otherwise.

The natal (birth) chart planets which are connected with the transit Moon during the currency of the Maha Dasha (Dasha), and Antar Dasha (Bukthi) of its aspecting planets will also confer their results to the native. ***These transit results are the essence of my research book 'Chandra Nadi'.***

The native will be assured of the results due to the Moon's transit.

The Transit of the Moon over the Sun in the natal (birth) chart: -

The Sun's Kharakathuvas and bhava significators will be the question and answer to a native who may shift or change in his residence.

As the moon is moving faster, the Karaka relatives of the Sun will undertake travel plans, especially the father. This travel results in good gains. The father/father-in-law will have a turbulent period where they could not make any proper decisions.

Karakathuva questions for example: -

Post, prestige, politics, the status of the son, the status of the father, the status of the father-in-law, and the status of self will be some questions that will crop up in the native's mind. Most of the questions raised with astrology consultants during this period of transit are based on the Karakathuvas of the Sun.

The transit of the Moon over natal (birth) Moon: -

When the transit Moon is approaching the natal (birth) chart Moon, the questions will be mostly based on the Karakathuvas of the Moon and its bhava significators.

The mother or mother-in-law will undertake journeys and there will be gains through it. The mother or mother-in-law will face a tough time and could not arrive at the correct decisions.

As Moon is responsible for mental disturbances, her transit over herself in the natal (birth) chart will increase intensive mental disturbances. When the native is not disturbed mentally, his/her mother or mother-in-law will be bothered.

In females, the uterus is denoted by the Moon they will face uterus-related problems and get cured. This transit intensifies the love feelings in ladies whereas reduces considerably amongst the gents.

Questions related to the Karakathuvas of the Moon: -

Depression, travel, the native's mother, the native's mother-in-law, situations leading to faults, or who is at fault? Status of the native? are the general questions. Even during astrological consultations, only these questions are put forth before the astrologer.

The transit of the Moon over natal (birth) Mars: -

1. This transit defines that of a watery planet over a heated planet which will last for just two and a quarter days only. During that two-and-a-quarter-day period, the native's mind will be driven to think about the Kasragathuvas of Mars and its significators only as the transit Moon will focus on the relates of Mars only.
2. The Karakathuvas of Mars may turn both positive and negative for the native. For example, House property, land, siblings, the status of the husband, vehicles, and treatment for the disease.
3. Those who have plans to build a house will either be fickle-minded or complete the building plan.
4. Those worried about their siblings will either worry more about them or e happy over their actions. In the case of married women, they will be fickle-minded about their husbands.
5. Those who borrowed against their land, house properties, and buildings will either be much worried about the loans or attempt to liquidate the loans.

The above results are interpreted both as positive and negative based on the Moon's transit over the natal (birth) chart Mars. When Mars is afflicted or with inimical planets these results will be negative and Mars is associated with friendlier planets the results will be on a positive note.

6. Brother/husband will undertake travel and will see benefits through it but will be fickle-minded during this period as they could not make any concrete decisions.
7. The native/the native's mother will strive to strengthen his/her base.

The transit of the Moon over natal (birth) Mercury: -

It is the convergence of wit and mind at the conscience end in transit.

The Mind will be focussed on the karakathuvas of Mercury, namely, education, love affairs, and their status, vacant land, agreements, documents, bank status, partnerships, joint venture, etc.,

Mercury, as an indicator of vacant land, will support those who would like to purchase vacant land.

Children/students will be forgetful and during this transit period of two-and-a quarter-day, those who are into love affairs and have afflicted Mercury in their natal (birth) chart should be careful.

It will be a duration of issues to ladies through ladies and gents through ladies.

As Mercury adopts hostile significators towards the Moon while it is the other way by the Moon, lovers will misunderstand between them as one is not in the good books of the other.

The conjunction of Rahu/Ketu/Mars during the transit of Moon over natal (birth) chart Mercury will entangle the native in legal affairs or force them to approach a police station.

Courtship with very young girls will lead to problems as Mercury indicates young girls.

Mercury is an indicator of business/trade and the Moon to mental instability, during this period inappropriate decisions in business/trade will result in heavy loss.

The transit of the Moon over natal (birth) Jupiter: –

This transit can be felt as a remarkable one as the native can venture into anything with confidence. Even in the case of deflected significators of Jupiter, the native will retain his qualities and face no hindrance to his respect. Child welfare activities can be undertaken.

The questions to the astrologers will mainly be based on children, family (tutelary) God, ways of economic and financial improvement, and auspicious events.

Childless couples can seek medical treatment to get progeny as their worries about remaining childless will be more during this transit. Doing spiritual merits during this transit will bring cheerful results in progeny. The questions to astrologers will be more based on the Karakathuvas of Jupiter.

The transit of the Moon over natal (birth) Venus: –

This is termed as the transit of an expenditure planet over the planet of means/money. During the currency of the period, greedy people will cross over, and afflicted Venus/Moon in the natal (birth) chart will result in unwanted expenditures. The Karakathuvas and bhava significators of Venus will be the question and answers during this transit.

Some of the Karakathuvas like Money due to the native, native's marriage, native's sister, and glands in the body are some of the questions that will be put forth to astrologers representing the Karakathuvas of Venus. There will be uncontrollable expenditures in succession.

The transit of the Moon over natal (birth) Saturn: –

It is the transit of the planet for travel over the planet of job/ business indicating that the native will undertake travel for job/

business purposes and make gains through it. There will be a change of place, mental stress, and uneasiness.

The Karakathuvas and bhava significators of Saturn will be the question and answer during the consultancy with the astrologer.

There will be a sexual attraction with elderly people and health will be spoilt if caution is not exercised.

Some questions relating to the Karakathuvas:

The native's job/business/profession, source of income? Family (tutelary) God and its missing worship? Why do no servants stick on permanently? Job prospects?

The above questions are posted to the astrologers during consultancy.

The transit of the Moon over natal (birth) Rahu: -

This transit can be termed as one travelling over a poison/poisonous creature. The Karakathuvas of Rahu and the bhava in which Rahu is posited will be the question and answer by the native during the consultancy with the astrologer.

1. The native will face severe problems and feel afraid.
2. The native will get a bad name.
3. The native will not receive any income.
4. Existing problems will aggravate or new problems will pop up.
5. The native will fear venom/poison.
6. Rahu denotes the intestine/rectum and the Moon denotes the body. Health will deteriorate due to the diseases to the intestine and any existing diseases will intensify.
7. The native will fear black magic and wade out, he will travel to find tantric remedies and feel depressed and lose money over it. During consultancy, only the Karakathuvas of Rahu is put forth to the astrologers **while approaching them during this transit with problems.**

The transit of the Moon over natal (birth) Ketu: –

The Karakathuvas of Ketu and bhava significators that Ketu posited will be the question and answers during the transit.

Some questions relating to the Karakathuvas:

1. Legal intricacies to the native.
2. Native subjected to separation.
3. Native entangled in unnecessary problems.
4. Fear of the native by facing severe problems. The natives suffer from intensified diseases.
5. The native will not receive any income.
6. The native will fear venom/poison and search for remedies, his travel to find tantric remedies and feel depressed and lose money over it. During consultancy, only the Karakathuvas of Rahu is put forth to the astrologers **while approaching them during this transit with problems.**

I have so far written 4 books based on the transit Moon's contact with natal (birth) planets and they were reprinted twice/thrice and published.

This is my faith in transit results. Your appreciation is the best reward for my hard work. As I had already written four volumes titled 'Chandra Nadi' based on the transit Moon, I have not discussed Moon at length here. Kindly read those books too and derive benefits. I welcome your opinions/doubts for clarification.

10.

MARS IN TRANSIT

Lord Mangala (Mars) Gayathri:

Ohm Veerathvajaya vidhmahe

Vigan hasthaaya deemahi

Thanno bhaumah prachodayath

Let Lord Mars bestow his blessings on us to understand all his

Karaka, bhava, and transit results

Transit Results: -

The transit of Mars over its friendlier planets the Karaka relations of Mars will be meritorious and will be impacted while moving over inimical planets.

11.

KARAKATHUVAS OF MARS

General Characteristics of Mars: -

Courage, anger, security, management, harsh words, rudeness, stubbornness, stubborn words, stubborn actions, excessive lust, rivalry, seriousness, serious thoughts, concerted efforts, physique, martial arts.

Mars in relationships/persons: -

Brothers and brothers-in-law in Male horoscopes (natal charts), husband and his brother in a female horoscope (natal chart), brother in common, younger siblings, blood relations, uniformed services, building architects, masters of martial arts (Karate), etc.,

Mars in parts of the body/disease: -

Blood, bone marrow, eyelids, bones, nails, teeth, vigour, twisted moustache, muscle strength, spleen-related diseases/deficiencies.

Places indicated by Mars: -

House, hospitals, research laboratories, thornbushes, Gyms, blasted areas, accident-prone zones, kitchen, south-west direction.

God/worship places denoted by Mars: -

Mars depicts Durga in female signs and Lord Muruga in male signs, demons in warrior postures, and fierce Gods.

Mars in products: -

Land, vehicles, weapons, machinery, machinery parts, coral, coral ornaments, explosives, explosive storehouse.

Mars as job/business pointer: -

All uniformed services (Police, Military, and all Defense services), Manager, Supervisors, Chef/Cooking, engineers, masters of martial arts, gym, soldiers, Chemicals, fertilizers, drug stores, barbers, dentists, metals, fire, sharp-edged weapons, mechanical, ground earth related jobs, agriculture, butchery, clock repair, dying factory, tailoring, leather industries, acts of bravery, products in red colour like a brick kiln, red chillies, commission business, knife, sickle, blood, surgery/operations, copper, coral business, etc., Mars acts as a commander and hence some cruel jobs are denoted by Mars.

12.

ROLE OF MARS IN MARITAL RELATIONS IN FEMALE HOROSCOPES

In female natal (birth) charts, Mars is the Karaka planet for the husband. The existence of blemishes caused by Mars is an unending debate.

According to our research, the blemish caused by the association of Mars with inimical planets rather than its occupation of a sign is more powerful to affect the native be a male or female. Mercury, Saturn, Rahu, and Ketu are inimical to Mars.

Mars associated with Mercury entangles the native in to love web before marriage to face problems.

Mars indicates courage and Rahu/Ketu induces blind actions. When Mars conjoins Rahu/Ketu, it gives rudeness and the native is propelled to act with rough courage resulting in evil than good.

Transit of Mars: -

Mars takes a day and a half to cross one degree and 45 days to pass over a sign. It takes approximately one year to go around the zodiac. In some years, it is stationed in a sign for about six months.

If the native is running Mars Maha Dasha (Dasha), Mars Antar Dasha (Bukthi), or Mars PrithyAntar Dasha (Anthram) during the **transit of Mars,** he will be experiencing good or bad results in excess. Otherwise, it will be comparatively less in quantum, but the native will realize Marsian benefits.

Transit of Mars over the Sun in the natal (birth) chart: -

It is the transit of a monthly planet over another monthly planet. There will not be any big results when the **Sun is not associated** with any Maha Dasha (Dasha), Antar Dasha (Bukthi), and or with inimical planets during the transit of Mars. As this is the transit of one heat planet over another heat planet, diseases related to body heat will bother the natives and those who are affected by diseases during this transit period affects progeny.

This can also be termed as a subordinate meeting a higher official in a fit of rage.

As Mars is the lord of Aries and the Sun exalts there, head injuries may be caused to the Karaka relations of the Sun whereas it will not affect brothers, the karaka relations of Mars.

Transit of Mars over the Moon in the natal (birth) Moon: -

Mars debilitates in Cancer owned by the Moon and the Moon debilitates in Scorpio owned by Mars. During this transit period, the husband of a female native will face humiliation.

Brothers of the native will face troubles in water due to the travel of monthly planet over daily planet representing water.

The native will be driven to act faster and face anger issues. Body temperature will increase. Affection towards siblings will increase.

Health issues will bother the native's mother/mother-in-law.

As the Moon denotes blood circulation and Mars denotes blood, blood pressure will increase showing variance in blood circulation.

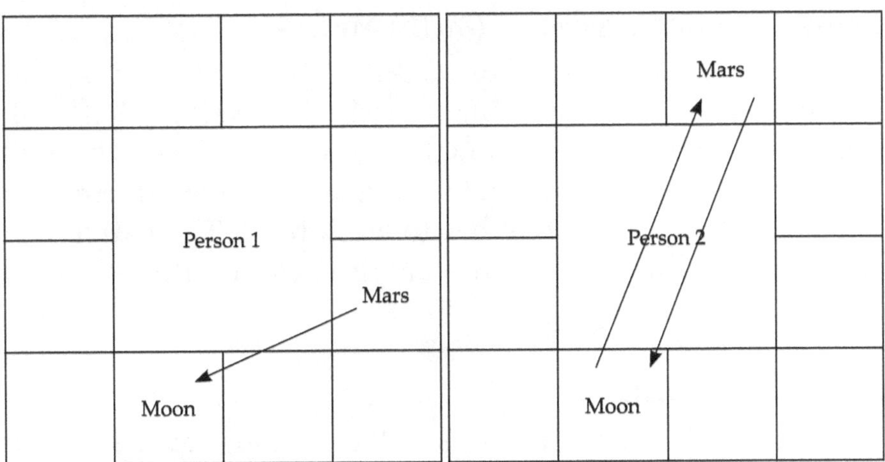

In both natal charts, the debilitated Moon in Scorpio receives the aspect of Mars. The natives were subjected to **lethal troubles in water twice**, the first one during the **transit of Mars aspect** to the natal Moon and the second one during the transit of **Mars over** the natal Moon.

While the first incident of trouble was the action of somebody, the second one happened due to the carelessness of the native.

Planetary aspects of Mars: –

The natal Mars that receives the aspect of natal Jupiter will not harm the native in a big way and extend only marginal impact.

On the contrary, the natal Mars in receipt of the aspects of the natal Saturn does not fail to extend its evil effects in transit and in turn, the natal Saturn receiving the inimical aspect of the natal Mars gives its evil impact during transit.

Mars afflicted by Rahu (Mars + Rahu) in the natal (birth) chart, travels with the same venom in its transit. It can be related to a person, born with a disease, carrying on as a patient throughout his life and wherever he goes.

A planet in transit exercises its results based on its acquisition of good/bad qualities/positions in the natal (birth) chart.

Transit of Mars over natal (birth) Mars: -

The administrative capacity of the native will increase but the association of natal Mars with inimical planets will change to maladministration resulting in a loss. The evil effects ascertained by the natal Mars will happen during the transit of Mars. The native has to work hard. The native will meet with multiple accidents or purchase multiple landed properties.

Detailed explanation: -

If this transit is related to Mars in the 4th house as the lord of the 4th house in the natal (birth) chart, it will affect the mother, comforts, pleasure, land and house property, and vehicles of the native. The association of the Moon here indicates the mother, ascendant/Lagna to health/comforts/pleasure, Venus to the vehicles, Mercury to vacant land, and Mars himself to house properties thus relating to the significators of Mars.

The placement of Mars in the sign of 7th bhava will indicate husband and in 3rd bhava to brothers. To get precise transit results, the placement of planets should be analyzed concerning their position in signs, aspects, conjunctions, asterisms, Maha Dasha (Dasha), and Antar Dasha (Bukthi). An astrologer can attain name and fame by giving results based on transit planets.

Due respect and name with fame can be received when results are revealed based on the conjunction/combination of two planets. When a deep analysis of a planet is attempted, the way of declaring the results will also improve.

Example: –

Birth chart

Rahu Mars	Birth		
Ascen- dant		Ketu	

Transit chart

		Ketu	
	Transit		
	Mars Rahu		

During the period of transit of Mars over the natal (birth) Mars…

In the native (birth) chart of a female native, Mars is placed in the 2nd house in an afflicted position (with Rahu). During transit, Mars is in Scorpio in the same afflicted stage conjoined with Rahu and throws its 4th aspect on the natal (birth) chart Mars. Her husband died in an accident.

The results as to the death of the husband should not be declared immediately on looking at the native chart. Initially, it should be revealed as an affliction of the Karaka relations of Mars to the native and as time passes by the technics of the transit results will improvise.

There will be doubts to choose among the various Karakathuvas of Mars in arriving at the results which can be ably decided with the support of the Maha Dasha (Dasha), Antar Dasha (Bukthi), and Prithyanthat Dasha (Anthram) lords. The incident/event will be very relevant to the significators of the lords of the Maha Dasha (Dasha), Antar Dasha (Bukthi), and PrithyAntar Dasha (Anthram).

As the female is married, this basic (birth) chart refers to her husband and had she not married, it would have referred to her brother.

Example: -

Ketu			
Mars	Birth		
	Ascendant	Rahu (Chitta)	

		Ketu	
	Transit		
	Mars Rahu		

The native has Rahu posited in the asterisms of Mars and receiving the 8th aspect of natal (birth) Mars and in transit, Mars is conjoined Rahu in Scorpio throwing its 4th aspect over natal (birth) Mars. The native met with an accident and underwent a surgery for bone fracture in the leg and now keeping in good health.

The placement and aspects of Mars are sure to affect the Karakathuvas of Mars.

In the natal chart, the evil placement of Rahu + Mars is invisible as Rahu is posited in the asterism of Mars (Chitta). It flared up when Rahu afflicted Mars in transit and threw its aspect on natal Mars.

The native suffered a fracture in the leg bone due to the transit of Mars but it would have been the hip bone had it been during the transit of Rahu as Mars is posited in Aquarius representing the legs and Rahu is placed in Virgo indicating hip bone. Thus, the relative planetary positions in their signs should be scrutinized for declaring the results.

Example: –

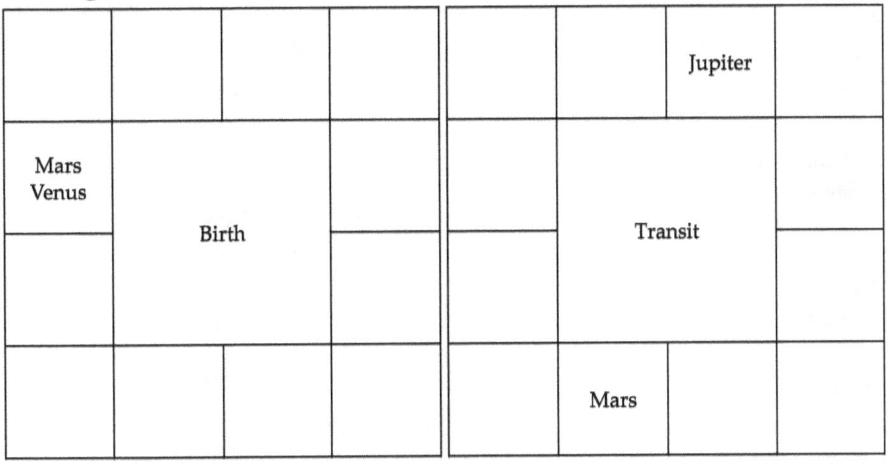

<table>
<tr><td></td><td></td><td></td><td></td><td></td><td>Jupiter</td><td></td></tr>
<tr><td>Mars
Venus</td><td rowspan="2">Birth</td><td></td><td></td><td rowspan="2">Transit</td><td></td><td></td></tr>
<tr><td></td><td></td><td>Mars</td><td></td></tr>
</table>

In the above natal (birth) chart, Venus is associated with Mars strengthening its benefic status and when transit Mars aspect this planetary combination from Scorpio, the benefic results will emerge. As the transit Mars acquires more beneficial strength due to the aspect of Jupiter, the benefic results will be in abundance.

In the transit chart, as Mars receives the aspect of Jupiter, the asterisms in which transit Jupiter posited vary the results extended. When Jupiter traverses the Kiruttiga star of the Sun, it will be authoritative, in Rohini star of the Moon with temptations and the requisite results in Mrigasira of Mars as for sure.

Example: -

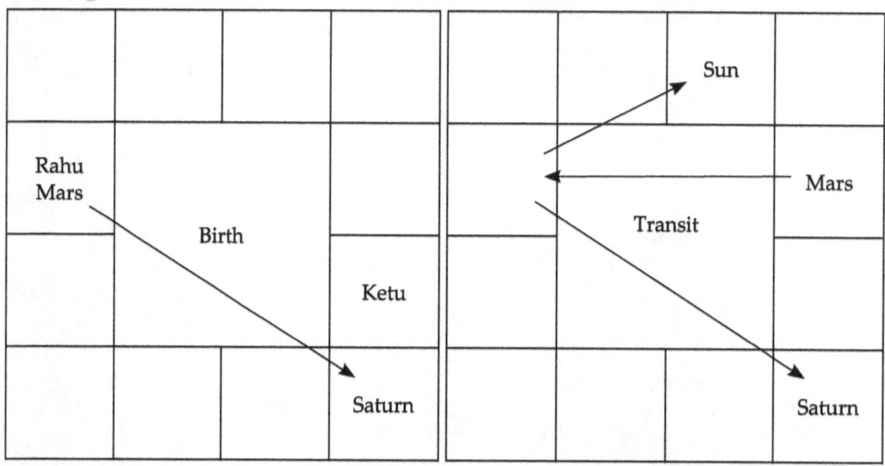

In the natal (birth) chart, Mars is in Aquarius conjoined with Rahu. Mars in transit from Cancer empowers the Aquarius sign through the 8th aspect.

Natal Mars in Aquarius stimulates the actions of planets posited in the signs through its 4th, 7th, and 8th aspects. This is like the servant extracting work from his master. The transit Mars aspect the transit Saturn who is over natal Saturn to cause the accident to the native and be hospitalised.

During his transit from Mars to Libra from cancer, he was discharged from the hospital to go home. When Mars moved to Scorpio, the Antar Dasha (Bukthi) of Saturn came to an end and hence the aspect of Mars from Scorpio to natal Mars in Aquarius did not give any untoward incidents and allowed the native to be at rest. He resumed his duties when Mars moved to Sagittarius.

When the planets in the natal (birth) charts are connected to the planets in transit and if they are the lords of the current Maha Dasha (Dasha), Antar Dasha (Bukthi), PrithyAntar Dasha (Anthram), then events will take place and those events will be of no importance or intense when they are not the lords of current Maha Dasha (Dasha), Antar Dasha (Bukthi), or Prithyanthat Dasha (Anthram).

The transit of Mars over the natal Mars and the asterisms in trikon (trines) empowers the natal Mars which means the Owner himself doing the work.

The aspect of the transiting Mars over the natal chart Mars implies the change in the character imparted by the natal Mars to the native and the acceleration of an event to occur.

The 4th aspect of Mars to a sign/planet imparts full strength to the planet/sign as the 4th aspect is considered as powerful by the Digbala possessed by Mars.

Notes: -

When a natal planet is conjoined by more than one planet, the planet in transit over them will be the combined result of all the planets. Hence an astrologer ought to know the combined planetary effects.

Transit of Mars over natal (birth) Mercury: -

Mercury denotes beau/lover and Mars indicates brother/husband hence this transit is construed to be a stagnation in marriage-related decisions.

As both are inimical against each other and fast-moving, the transit of the planets is to be followed thoroughly.

This transit gives events to sick patients and youth. It gives beneficial results to land dealers/promoters and those in the banking sector. (Mercury denotes land and banking).

Those who own land could venture into building construction. Lovers can get married. It is a testing time for young girls.

This transit is like enemies barging into the house and beating. During this transit, lovers attempt to elope.

Transit of Mars over natal (birth) Jupiter: -

This is the transit of a monthly planet over a yearly planet and both are friendlier planets. As both Jupiter and Mars are lords of trines to each other they will extend good results to the natives rather than evil.

As Mars is travelling over the planet of wealth (money) Jupiter, Karakathuvas of Mars cause auspicious events and the native will be fond of carbohydrate food.

The native will be fond of ancestral properties and will seek funds to renovate them. New properties will be acquired and income will be sourced through land and house properties.

The native will go in search of people in the hierarchy and will benefit through their meetings.

In female horoscopy who is into separation, the husband will visit to see his children.

Jupiter denotes muscles and Mars to twisting as their Karakathuvas, indicating that the native will face muscle contraction/muscle twisting causing pain.

Transit of Mars over natal (birth) Venus: -

This refers to the meeting of two Kalathra Karaka lords as both husband and wife will be more attracted towards each other. The husband who is separated from his wife will be willing to unite with his wife. During the currency of this transit, if no connections with inimical planets Rahu/Ketu exists, the couples in separation will unite back.

If the properties are to be disposed of to make money, this transit will put through the transaction and money will fructify. (Money – Venus, property – Mars) Brother/husband will realize money.

Any existing confrontation between brother and sister will be amicably settled.

If Venus and Mars are connected to Rahu/Ketu in the natal chart, the native may have to go to his sister relating to the partition of properties or his wife's relations due to problems. Both will aggravate the problems.

The above problems will be negated and good results can be enjoyed had Venus and Mars not connected to Rahu/Ketu.

Beneficial results can be derived if Venus and Mars are connected to Jupiter.

Vehicular and logistics comforts can be enjoyed as both Venus and Mars are Karakas for Vehicles, but their association with inimical/malefic planets will result in vehicular accidents. The position of Venus as 'Maragadhipathi' or 'Bhadagathipathi' as indicators of the 2nd /7th house lord or 11th, 9th, 7th, for Moveable, Fixed, common ascendants respectively, then this transit period will cause vehicular accidents and caution should be exercised.

Note: – Malefic/inimical planets:

Both Malefic and Inimical are two different characteristics. The Sun is a natural malefic but it is friendlier to Mars and treats Saturn and Venus as enemies. This difference should be clearly understood in terming the results during transit.

Transit of Mars over natal (birth) Saturn: –

This is the transit of the lord of the *8th house 'Ashtamathipathi' Mars to 'Kalapurusha'* (Time-personified) ascendant/Lagna Aries/Mesha over *evil 11th house 'Bhadagathipathi' Saturn to 'Kalapurusha'* (Time-personified) and that of two **inimical planets to one another**. As this transit lasts only for a short duration of one month (transit of Monthly planet Mars over a yearly planet Saturn), the good and bad results will not continue for long. But if this happens to be the Maha Dasha (Dasha), Antar Dasha (Bukthi), or PrithyAntar Dasha (Anthram) of either of the planets, then this transit should be feared about giving at least one bad incident/event.

The connection of these two planets in the natal (birth) chart indicates certain accidents and if the transit period happens to be the Maha Dasha (Dasha), Antar Dasha (Bukthi), PrithyAntar Dasha (Anthram) of the lethal (Maraka), evil (Badaga) effects the accidents will be severe and major resulting in death.

Integration of these two, 11th house Saturn as bhadagathipathi and 8th house Mars as ashtamadhipathi, in a sign or their aspect of a sign, will cause accidents.

Saturn as a 'karmic' planet indicates 'karmic' enemies and Mars as courage defines the increased strength of enemies. It is needless to win over 'karmic' enemies as over some time the attitude/character of the enemies will change.

This transit may press for updating/renewing old machinery and purchasing new ones for industrial development.

This transit will give mixed results of both good and bad depending upon the bhava indication of the current Maha Dasha (Dasha), Antar Dasha (Bukthi) and the sign in which the transit takes place.

This transit indicates the accidents and lethal events that are bound to happen. Such accidents and lethal events should have been indicated in the natal (birth) chart to take place during transit. It will impact the sign in which both these planets converge and cause damages and injuries to the parts of the body indicated by the signs aspected by these two planets. When the planets are associated with Rahu/Ketu, surgeries need to be carried out.

Example: –

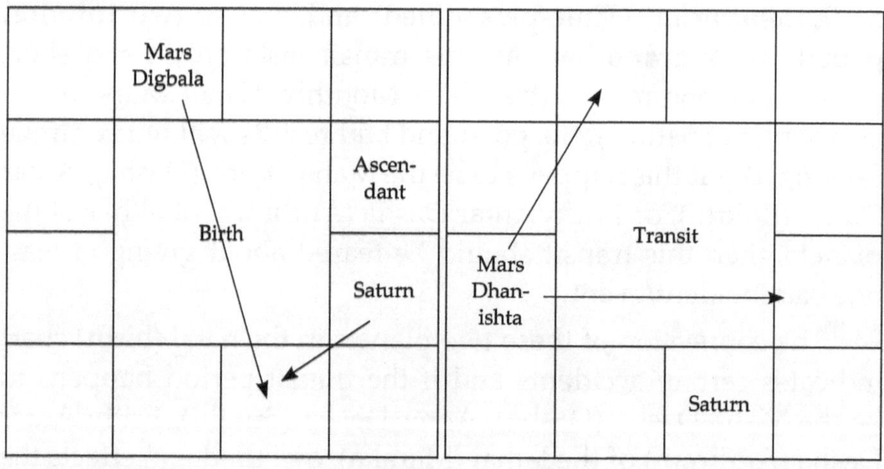

In the above chart, Mars is posited in Aries with Digbala (10th house of ascendant) and aspects Libra – the 4th house of comfort to Cancer ascendant. Saturn in Leo throws its 3rd aspect on Libra. As both inimical planets aspect the 4th house of comfort, the native is accident-prone and the time of the accident will be indicated by the transit planetary position.

Transit Mars aspects natal Mars through its 4th aspect and natal Saturn through its 8th aspect which is considered special because Mars is transiting in its asterism Dhanishta with exalted strength in Capricorn, a house owned by Saturn. The connectivity with the natal planets by the transit of Mars is established sign-wise and star-wise show causing the impact to Libra by Saturn and Mars. Transit of both the planets in the signs aspected by them gives good or bad results in a big way.

As the native had Cancer as his ascendant and Mars in 'Digbala' (angular strength), he established an engineering industry. He met with an accident during this transit period.

Example: -

<table>
<tr><td></td><td></td><td></td><td></td></tr>
<tr><td>Saturn</td><td colspan="2" rowspan="2">Birth</td><td></td></tr>
<tr><td></td><td>Mars</td></tr>
<tr><td></td><td></td><td></td><td></td></tr>
</table>

<table>
<tr><td></td><td></td><td></td><td></td></tr>
<tr><td>Mars</td><td colspan="2" rowspan="2">Transit</td><td></td></tr>
<tr><td></td><td></td></tr>
<tr><td></td><td></td><td></td><td></td></tr>
</table>

During the transit of Mars over the natal (birth) chart Saturn, the native approached his brother for business and prospered, as Mars in Leo's aspect Saturn in Aquarius indicates he will lose or gain business through his brother, the Karaka of Mars.

Consideration of the above chart as that of a female:

Here Mars represents the husband and Saturn as his job. The husband of the female got a job as a driver who is not so agile and was active only a few months in a year. When the reason for his behaviour is analyzed, he was found to be active only during the transit of Mars and Saturn passing over or associated with natal (birth) Mars or Saturn.

She has not objected when she was told that her husband earns a handful when engaged in a job related to the Karaka of Mars only and facing problems in any other job he is engaged in.

When a person is engaged in the job/business projected/ identified by the combination of two inimical planets, he is not troubled/bothered by those inimical planets but rather supports him.

When Mars is exalted in a natal (birth) chart: -

Transit Mars will traverse each house/sign with its exalted power and with utmost power in his exalted house – Capricorn. It is something like a soldier conferred with the powers of a Commander/Chief. while traversing in the debilitated house of Cancer his exalted powers will not work and he will remain inactive, which can be compared to a Commander/Chief degraded to work as a Soldier.

When Mars is debilitated in a natal (birth) chart: -

Transit Mars will traverse each house/sign with debilitated powers and while passing over debilitated house Cancer, it will be still worse. In the exalted house, he will travel without debilitated powers and will remain neutral.

When Mars is Combust in a natal (birth) chart: -

In transit Mars will travel with combust power.

Rahu/Ketu afflicted Mars in the natal (birth) chart: -

When Mars is afflicted by the evil nodes Rahu/Ketu in the natal (birth) chart, he will travel with his affliction in transit. The transit of Mars over benefic planets will not allow any good events to happen or afflict the Karakathuvas of the benefic planets.

Transit of Rahu/Ketu afflicted Mars over inimical planets will cause evil incidents or the death of the native.

Example: -

Moon		Saturn	
Mars	Birth		Ketu
Rahu			Venus
	Jupiter		Sun Mercury

Virtues	Ruling	Artistic Excellence	Knowledge
Admin	Transit		Debility Problems
Exaltation Problems Virtues			Admin
Virtues	Ruling	Artistic Excellence	Knowledge

Natal Mars is posited in Aquarius.

Transit of Mars in Aquarius: -

During its transit in Aquarius, Mars will display results as a combined source of natal Mars and Leo Venus.

Transit of Mars in Pisces: -

During the transit of Mars in Pisces, the native Mars will perform as the Moon who received the combined aspect of Jupiter, Sun and Mercury.

From the transit of Mars, natal Mars acquires the significators of the Moon's temptation, the magnanimity of Jupiter, the intellectual thoughts of Mercury, and the administrative capacity of the Sun.

Transit of Mars in Aries: -

As there are no Planets in Aries, the natal Mars acquires Ruling strength during the transit of Mars in Aries.

Transit of Mars in Taurus: -

The transit Mars in Taurus acquires strength from Saturn in Taurus who receives the aspect of Jupiter in Scorpio and Mars in Aquarius and confers it to the natal Mars in Aquarius. The native will escape from any possible accidents and the elder brother of the native will be doing a nice job earning a sizeable income.

Transit of Mars in Gemini: -

The transit of Mars in Gemini by receiving the trikon connection of natal Mars in Aquarius coupled with the significators of Mercury, the lord of Gemini confers the foretelling of events to natal Mars.

Transit of Mars in Cancer: -

Transit Mars will confer the strength acquired by its conjunction with Ketu and Jupiter's aspect to natal Mars. As the transit Mars is debilitated, it will have a mean character. The native will be from unwanted fears and legal complications.

Transit of Mars in Leo: -

Transit Mars will confer the results of the combined strength of natal Venus and the aspect of natal Mars to Venus along with the characters of Venus and Mars. As Mars is traversing in a hot sign, natal Mars has a heated temperament. The native will exhibit honest qualities.

Transit Mars in Virgo: -

Transit Mars will confer the significators and character of Mercury, Sun, and Moon to natal Mars. The natal Mercury will empower the native with knowledge during this transit.

Transit Mars in Leo: -

Transit Mars will confer the significators of Venus and the combined impact of the trikon (trine) effects of natal Mars in Aquarius to Mars.

Transit of Mars in Scorpio: -

Transit Mars will confer the benefits of its combination with natal Jupiter along with its significators and that of natal Saturn who aspect Scorpio sign to natal Mars. Hence the natal Mars will possess the generosity, significators and qualities of Jupiter. Even though Mars is not ruling, it will have the qualities and capabilities of ruling when Mars transit over Scorpio.

Transit of Mars in Sagittarius: -

During this period of transit, Mars will confer the significators, generosity, and qualities of Jupiter to natal Mars.

Transit of Mars in Capricorn: -

Mars in transit will confer the impact of natal Rahu and dispositions of exalted Mars to natal Mars.

Even when natal Mars is not in an exalted position, as the transit Mars is exalted it will confer the actions and significators of exalted effect to natal Mars. The transit Mars will face crisis and fear.

Transit Mars concerning other planets in transit: -

Transit Mars attains weakness or strength depending on other transiting planets. As mentioned above, all other planetary transits should be reckoned with in arriving at precise results.

Relating the transit of Mars to that of a brother – a Karakathuva of Mars: -

The transit Mars is responsible for the change in character and behaviour of the brother of the native remaining active, mighty, stubborn, and kind for some time and dull, weak, and inactive during other times alternatively.

Through research…

When the strength of a planet is assessed on the above lines, the quality of the results predicted will be extraordinary is what I inferred from my research. Kindly experiment with the relativity theory of transit based on the above and enjoy the results.

Transit of Mars over natal (birth) Rahu: -

The implication of the travel of a monthly planet over that of a yearly planet and the convergence of two inimical against each other in transit. The native could perform less auspicious events and face more disadvantageous situations and bad incidents. This transit adds fuel to already burning anger in a person and most people lose their potential life during this transit period unable to bear the brunt.

In Men…

Transit of Mars over Rahu implies that the brother of the native looks for bad company and should be cautious. During the transit, there may be attempts to pledge, pawn or gamble using land and house properties. Here Mars denotes house/land and Rahu to pledging activities.

In Women…

The native's brother or husband will be pushed into bad company/ notorious people. During the transit, there may be attempts to pledge, pawn or gamble using land and house properties. The native's husband will meet with accidents.

In Children…

As Mars is transiting over Rahu, any childish activities will result in serious repercussions which may even be an accident insisting on the need for caution. Exercising control and care in food and diet will save from fever and diseases.

Rahu refers to perversity and Mars to sports and games.

In General: -

During the transit of 'Kalathra Karaka' Mars over the 'Karaka' for delay/blockade Rahu, there will be delay or deferment of marriage or instigate separation of husband and wife.

The Bride or Groom will reject each other in a sudden instant and stop the marriage during this transit period.

It will be a period when girls will commit further mistakes to cover the past unscrupulous incidents.

Rahu denotes the boundary and Mars to place/land. As the lord of the land travel over the lord of the boundary, it will cause problems in construction beyond approved plans and faulty land measurements. House construction proposals during this transit do not yield good/desired results.

The husband/brother will be inclined towards sexual pleasures and those who lack energy will resort to medicines.

This transit is not considered as good as it inflicts death on the husband/brother.

Differentiation of transit: -

The transit of Mars over Rahu is like getting pierced by thorns or receiving cuts for some reason.

The transit of Rahu over is like hurting oneself with knife cuts/sharp tools/weapons, and the native will be alone in this case and none can be blamed for his actions.

When this is related to Maha Dasha (Dasha), and Antar Dasha (Bukthi), the native will be attacked by lethal/sharp weapons receiving cuts. An individual or a group will be involved in this case against whom legal actions can be initiated.

During the course of the transit of Mars over natal Rahu, intensive problems regarding boundaries in the land purchased and partition-related problems will flare up.

Double transit period: -

Given below is an event that occurred during the transit of Mars over natal (birth) Jupiter and natal (birth) Rahu in conjunction. This should be noted as two transits are involved in it.

During the transit of Mars over natal (birth) Jupiter the native using his friend's money bought some lands at a cheaper price and later sold them for a good sum. He repeated the process as he made a good profit in the deal. His greed drove him to buy more land. During the transit of Mars over natal (birth) Rahu he was caught in financial problems and lost his entire earnings from past deals. He was left with debt even after selling his entire land holdings. To set off his dues, he sold not only his portion but that of his brother too without giving him his due share. Now he has obviated from his hometown.

Those who have Mars and Rahu combination in their natal (birth) chart should not commit mistakes in dealing with the Karaka-related issues of Mars/Rahu. A person with Rahu + Mars in his natal (birth) chart should not be greedy in purchasing land as he will be financially victimised if he could not sell the land so purchased when in crisis.

When will be he victimised?

The native will be victimised during the transit of Mars over natal (birth) Rahu or when Rahu transit over natal (birth) Mars.

Persons with such natal combinations are advised to purchase lands with their excessive funds and when they do not need to sell.

Transit of Mars over natal (birth) Ketu: -

It resembles the native's attempts to stabilize by approaching a legal advisor. The native will be punished by either natal (birth) Ketu or transit Mars – whosoever – in the lead and/or both.

This is the transit of a monthly planet Mars over a yearly planet Ketu. The two planets, Mars and Ketu, who are inimical to each other join together to punish the native. There will be legal implications in land and house properties.

Transit Mars who is the Karaka for house and landed properties indicates that they will be voluntarily entangled in legal issues.

The situation to purchase litigated properties will emerge and when such litigated properties are bought problems will follow which will take a long time to settle. Those who have such combinations should avoid buying land as they are inviting problems.

During this transit, the egoism of the native will surface and he will have undue courage.

For women: -

If there exists a problem between husband and wife, this transit will flare up forcing them to seek legal remedies or separation before a bench of elders or judiciary. When the problems are not properly and patiently handled, it will result in complications.

Example: –

In the below-given chart, Ketu is in Pisces in Uthra-Bhadra, the asterism of Saturn and Rahu is in Virgo, a sign owned by Mercury. Transit of Mars in the asterism of Saturn pushes him to collide with Ketu and his transit in the star Revathi of Mercury will see him bleeding and impacted by Rahu in Virgo.

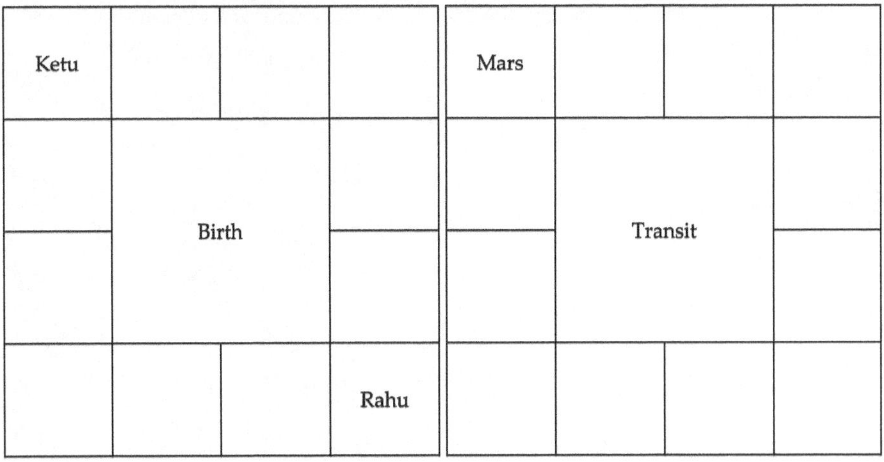

Ketu					Mars			
		Birth					Transit	
			Rahu					

The situation to purchase litigated properties will emerge and when such litigated properties are bought problems will follow which will take a long time to settle.

Those who have such combinations should avoid buying land as they are inviting problems.

A person came to consult regarding the purchase of landed property which was offered at a very low price. He was advised to go for the deal after transit Mars cross over natal (birth) Ketu.

But he never listened to what I said. After paying about 80% advance amount, he learnt about the encumbrances in the property and hence could not get it registered. After a lapse of four years, he got back only 25% of the advance amount paid by him. Planets passing over Ketu will involve voluntary involvement in the problems.

Notes: –

While the problems cropping up during the transit of Mars over natal (birth) Ketu can be avoided, the one arising out during the transit of Ketu over natal (birth) Mars could not be avoided and has to be suffered.

13.

MERCURY IN TRANSIT

Lord Buda (Mercury) Gayathri:

Ohm Gajathvajaya vidhmahe

Suka hasthaya deemahi

Thanno Budha prachodath

Let Lord Mercury bestow his blessings on us to understand all his

Karaka, bhava, and transit results

Transit Results: –

The transit of Mercury over its friendlier planets the Karaka relations of Mercury will be meritorious and will be impacted while moving over inimical planets. Mercury wins over all planets.

14.

KARAKATHUVAS OF MERCURY

Mercury in General: -

Accountant, knowledge, dual nature, a eunuch in gender, indirect answers, escapism, minute problems. When a question arises as to what results to say based on Mercury, it helps surreptitiously to give special and minute astrological predictions.

Mercury in relations/persons: -

Maternal uncle, uncle, younger sister, beau, lover, friends, assistants/helpers.

Mercury in parts of the body/feelings: -

Skin, nervous system, and desires of a person.

Mercury in places: -

Schools, windows, Banks, conference halls, shelves, libraries, tables, society, collection centres, accounting zones, assemblies of educationists, vacant land, newspaper offices, and astrology centres.

Mercury as God:

Lord Maha Vishnu, all forms of Lord Vishnu, Saptha Kannimar (Seven spinsters) Kannimars, Kandarva kannimars, Kandarvas (demons)

Mercury in things/products: -

Materials used in education and those required to acquire knowledge.

Mercury in job/business: -

Astrology, medical treatment, occult sciences, travel related, newspaper, lawyer, printing, stamp sales, document writing, educational institutions and education related, vehicle registration, traffic regulation, entertainment, wit, dance, dopes, green colour products, grains and cereals sale, oratory skill, music.

Mercury in marital relations: -

Mercury denotes intelligence. All business/jobs related to accounts and maths, Banks, Bank staff and officials, all accounting subsects, preachers, pastors, astrologers, teachers, educationalists, researchers, plot sellers, actors, artists, comedians, speakers, book writers, booksellers, book publishers, singers, entertainers, music recordings, musicians, music booksellers, accountants, clerk, secretaries, editors, auditors, postman, translation job, beau, and lovers.

When Mercury is alone, it never affects but the problems will accrue when it conjoins its inimical planets, Mars, Moon, and Rahu/Ketu.

Mercury during Transit: -

Mercury takes 3 days, and 18 hours or approximately 90 hours. Mercury retrogrades for 21 days every three months. It will be combusted for 22 days.

Mercury takes approximately one month to cross over a sign and takes approximately one year to complete the zodiac.

During the transit of Mercury, if the native is running Mercury Maha Dasha (Dasha), Antar Dasha (Bukthi), and PrithyAntar Dasha (Anthram), then the results will be good or bad in abundance, and less when not.

Transit of Mercury is sure to confer its benefits.

Transit Mercury over natal (birth) Sun: -

Adults when open up to their parents, their maximum problems will be solved. During this period if the passive talk is initiated cordially and kindly with very young adult girls, many problems and difficulties they were about to face will not surface and can be forbidden. **This will prevent young children obviate or go missing from home.** The Karaka relations of the Sun will benefit from the Karaka of the Mercury. For example, the native's father will gain through land dealings of purchase and sale.

Transit of Mercury over natal (birth) Moon: -

1. This will aggravate the already mentally retarded.
2. Aspect of the Jupiter extends memory power. The transit will bring humiliation.

Transit of Mercury over natal (birth) Mars: -

Women will be bothered much by this transit. This period will prove hectic for those who have already committed some mistakes/ errors and temptations will lure them. The Brother/husband of the female will have extramarital affairs causing disharmony in life. As Karaka for brother Mars and Karaka for friend Mercury is connected, misunderstandings between brothers and friends will flare up.

In the case of a female native, her beau (lover) will quarrel with her husband or brother and during this transit, if the 2nd house is connected to Saturn, then excessive humiliation will result. If Mars or Mercury possess the significators of the 3rd, and 8th houses, then it will be a period of elopement with lover/ beau. A thorough scrutiny is required before declaring the results.

Those who are into mathematical and scientific research, competitors, and intellectuals will gain through this transit.

Transit Mercury over natal (birth) Mercury: -

1. A good time to get good friends.
2. It is a nice time to meet intellectuals and curiosity to learn will be more.

Transit of Mercury over natal (birth) Jupiter: -

Transit of a monthly benefic over a yearly benefic. There will be no bad impacts. Even if some significators of Jupiter are in affliction, it will not bother the native much. If the transit period happens to be the Maha Dasha (Dasha), Antar Dasha (Bukthi) of Jupiter or Mercury then according to their benefic significators, the best results will be conferred by them.

1. A good time to get good friends.
2. A good time for learners.

Transit of Mercury over natal (birth) Venus: -

This refers to the transit of a monthly planet over a monthly planet. Both are very soft and sattvic planets. A result conferred by them will last for generations. Ladies will get beaus close to their hearts.

An association of good friends will be there. The transit of Mercury in a male sign will associate male friends and in a female sign will bring in female friends. Both gents and ladies will get increased income and this excessive income may be invested in vacant land.

When Mercury is not afflicted in the natal (birth) chart, it does not give evil results and extends evil results when afflicted.

If Venus is associated with Rahu/Ketu in the natal (birth) chart, the transit of Mercury over Venus will give evil results relating to the Karaka, and bhava significators.

Example: -

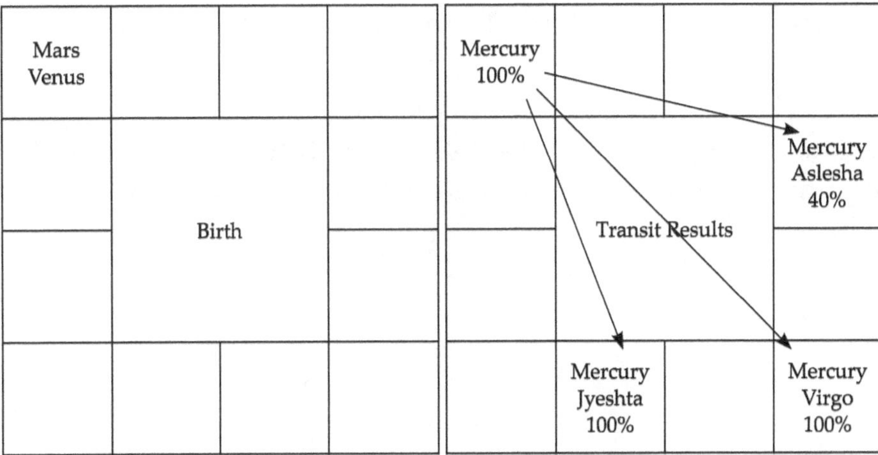

During the transit of Mercury over natal (birth) Mars, and exalted Venus in the natal (birth) chart the native approached to know about his wife's activities. He was advised not to enquire about anything related to illicit relations with his wife till Mercury Passover Pisces as she will answer boldly with the support of her beau and to make inquire after that. But he did not listen and made enquiries only to get a bold answer from his wife causing embarrassment. (Mercury when alone is a coward but becomes brave when associated with Mars).

The transit of Mercury over natal (birth) Mars and natal (birth) Venus induces illicit marital relations and forces misbehaviour making life miserable if caution is not exercised. **Though Mercury is soft and gentle, the evil results caused by it will be very hard.**

If a transiting planet has its star (asterism) in the sign in which it is transiting, it gains natural strength. The strength gained will be more if any other planet is posited in the star of the transiting planet which will be given powerful results.

Transit of Mercury over natal (birth) Saturn: -

It is the transit of a monthly planet over a yearly planet indicating the business trader over the industrial manufacturer.

During this period every action will be based on business thoughts. Real estate sellers will make a good harvest. Only Saturn's placement in 8th or 12th from the ascendant gives problems and mental stress.

As both Saturn and Mercury belong to the eunuch category, sexual feelings will be subsidised. If both have 3rd, 7th, and 11th significators and if the transit is over those bhavas, it will be at a critical level.

Example: –

<table>
<tr><td></td><td></td><td></td><td></td><td></td><td></td><td></td><td>Art</td></tr>
<tr><td></td><td colspan="2" rowspan="2" align="center">Birth</td><td></td><td></td><td colspan="2" rowspan="2" align="center">Transit</td><td></td></tr>
<tr><td></td><td></td><td></td><td></td></tr>
<tr><td></td><td></td><td>Saturn</td><td></td><td></td><td></td><td></td><td>Mercury Business</td></tr>
</table>

The native of the above natal chart made a big success in vacant land/plot sales during the Saturn Maha Dasha (Dasha), and Mercury Antar Dasha (Bukthi). The Virgo sign refers to vacant land business. Consultants and advisors make a big buck without big investments in the Karaka of Saturn during this transit. Many big ventures take off only during this transit period.

Transit of Mercury over natal (birth) Rahu: –

It is considered an evil period as the transit of a soft, sattvic planet over a malefic and inimical planet. This may bring change in the habits and attitudes of the native's younger siblings which necessitates caution in handling them. Relations referred to by the Karaka of Mercury will turn hostile. The association of Mercury and Rahu in the natal chart will enhance the evil results during the transit of Mercury based on the current Maha Dasha (Dasha), and Antar Dasha (Bukthi).

This transit increases the marketing skills as elaborate talking with the customers.

The transit of Mercury over Rahu kindles interest in occult sciences like mantric, tantric, and alchemy which results in the aftermath. A disaster can be foretold if this transit is associated with the current Maha Dasha (Dasha), Antar Dasha (Bukthi) happens to be that of Rahu/Mercury.

Many people who wanted to make a big buck with smaller investments are mentally affected or committed suicide during this transit period pressing the need for caution.

As Arudra asterism (star) owned by Rahu is in Mercury's Gemini sign, any effort indulged by Mercury associated with Rahu is relatively easier compared to Mercury's association with Ketu. Mercury which insists on fairness while associating with Ketu does not insist or remains silent when associated with Rahu.

Transit of Mercury over natal (birth) Ketu: -

It is considered an evil period as the transit of a soft, sattvic planet over a malefic and inimical planet. Relations referred to by the Karaka of Mercury will have legal complications or the native will voluntarily fix himself in legal issues. The association of Mercury and Ketu in the natal chart will enhance the evil results during the transit of Mercury based on the current Maha Dasha (Dasha), and Antar Dasha (Bukthi).

The transit of Mercury over Ketu kindles interest in occult sciences like mantric, tantric, and alchemy which results in the aftermath. A disaster can be foretold if this transit is associated with the current Maha Dasha (Dasha), Antar Dasha (Bukthi) happens to be that of Ketu/Mercury.

Many people who wanted to make a big buck with smaller investments are mentally affected or committed suicide during this transit period pressing the need for caution.

The native talk over more than required will result in misunderstanding and difficulties. As Mercury refers to friends and Ketu to differences of opinion, misunderstanding with even close friends will be a reality.

Notes: -

The transit of two inimical planets reveals evil results as a rule. But in the case of Mercury, the evil results will not be explicit but will happen.

15.

JUPITER IN TRANSIT

Lord Guru (Jupiter) Gayathri:

Ohm Gurudevaaya vidhmahe

Parabrahmaya deemahi

Thanno Guruh prachodath

Let Lord Jupiter bestow his blessings on us to understand all his Karaka, bhava, and transit results

Transit Results: –

With the transit of Jupiter over its friendlier planets, the Karaka relations of Jupiter will be meritorious and will be impacted while moving over inimical planets.

16.

THE KARAKATHUVAS OF JUPITER

Jupiter in General: -

All auspicious effects, deeds, significators, honesty, discipline, and all meritorious actions are the Karakathuvas of Jupiter. Jupiter's by aspect purifies a planet. The aspect of Jupiter is more beneficial than its association/combination with a planet.

Jupiter in relations/persons: -

Great grandfather, children, esteemed and respectable, wealthy people.

Jupiter in parts of the body/feelings: -

Brain, liver functions, liver, gall bladder, tumours in the body, the function of the heart, function of boneless structures.

Jupiter in places: -

Agraharam (places where brahmins reside), children's play area, lockers, gold, places where auspicious things/materials or kept. Pooja places where brahmins do rituals.

Jupiter as God: -

Ritually observed Gods, family (tutelary) Gods.

Jupiter in articles/products: -

Gold, auspicious materials/things.

Jupiter in business: -

Turmeric business, lawyers, judges, brokers, pundits, purohits, ritual performers, temple priests, Doctors, Banking businesses/employment, money lenders, provision stores, and textile businesses. Vedanta, Siddhartha, religious preaching, textile business, teaching, Cashiers where money is handled, spiritually associated business, treatise related, gold business, chit funds, life insurance corporation, philanthropy, actions involving a compromise.

Jupiter in marital life: -

Jupiter is the indicator of domestic pleasure through the wife to husband and husband to wife. It is good to have Jupiter's association or aspect of Mars in female horoscopes/natal charts. Similarly, it will be good if Jupiter is associated with or aspect of Venus or associated with the 7th lord or aspect of the 7th lord in the natal chart/horoscope of a male. In the absence of the above combinations, it will be mechanical marriage life.

Transit of Jupiter: -

As Jupiter is a yearly planet, the results experienced by Jupiter's transit will be for a longer duration and as planets inimical to Jupiter are less in number, auspicious results given by Jupiter will be more than evil. The number of people who experience good results is more than those who experienced evil results.

Jupiter takes 12 days to pass over one degree of the zodiac and 40 days and 14 hours over one past. of an asterism (star). He moves 5' 55" a day, takes a year to pass over a sign and 12 years to complete a circle of the zodiac.

Transit of Jupiter over natal (birth) Sun: -

This is the transit of a spiritual yearly planet over the monthly planet representing the Soul thereby inducing spirituality. This gives good auspicious results to the native and brings respect and status to the father. During this period Opinions, findings and research results can be explained to the Government and receive accolades and rewards. The father and the son who lived in separation can stand united.

Here separation of the father and son can be presumed as one at home and the other in the military or one at home and the other staying in a hostel. This union is after separation on good terms. (Separation due to bitterness will be indicated by the association of Rahu/Ketu with these planets).

Transit of Jupiter over natal (birth) Moon: -

The results should be declared based on Jupiter's position concerning the position of the sign in which the natal (birth) Moon is posited.

If transit Jupiter finds a planet in the sign of its travel, the result of the combination of that planet with Jupiter and that of the placement of Jupiter from the Moon should be packed together.

Jupiter in the 1st house from the Moon:

This is termed as *'Jupiter at birth'* an evil position causing humiliation in the life of the native. Change of place is imminent. Many families have faded away due to humiliation and some have died during this transit. If this transit occurs during the Maha Dasha (Dasha), Antar Dasha (Bukthi) of Jupiter or Moon it will cause frustration and dejection in life.

Jupiter in the 2nd house from the Moon:

The native will be neglected by his/her mother. Some may be forced to migrate from their native place but will prosper in the new place.

Jupiter in the 3rd house from the Moon:

There will be ignominy in marriage issues. Tussles with siblings will prevail. If this happens to be the Maha Dasha (Dasha) of Jupiter/Moon, it will cause death.

Jupiter in the 4ᵗʰ house from the Moon:

During this period properties may be lost to relations. The possibility of accidents should be averted by exercising caution.

Jupiter in the 5ᵗʰ house from the Moon:

Auspicious events will take place.

Jupiter in the 6ᵗʰ house from the Moon:

Possibility of accidents. Should be careful.

Jupiter in the 7ᵗʰ house from the Moon:

Auspicious events will take place.

Jupiter in the 8ᵗʰ house from the Moon:

The name will be spoilt due to bad actions and events. The native will be subjected to betrayal.

Jupiter in the 9ᵗʰ house from the Moon:

Auspicious events will take place.

Jupiter in the 10ᵗʰ house from the Moon:

The native will feel bitterness in his/her job/profession, and may even lose his/her job/profession, may not he/she be duly entitled. This transit will cause bitterness in every source of income.

It is a proverb that a **Brahmin (Jupiter) alone in the 10ᵗʰ house causes agony. This transit will cause havoc in the family life if the native is currently running Maha Dasha (Dasha) of Jupiter/Moon.**

Jupiter in the 11ᵗʰ house from the Moon:

Auspicious events will take place.

Jupiter in the 12ᵗʰ house from the Moon:

Medical expenses will increase during this transit.

		Saturn				Jupiter	
	Birth				Transit		
	Moon						

In the above natal (birth) chart, Saturn is in Taurus, and Moon is in Libra. The transit of Jupiter in Taurus marks its 8th house position to the natal (birth) Moon.

But Saturn is present in Taurus, the yoga karaka or the lord of boons for Taurus. Hence the impact of Jupiter in the 8th house on the Moon will rather give benefic results than evil and eventually forbid any lethal events, restricting the 8th house effects of Jupiter. However, there will be some impact which will not be serious.

This is the difference between general predictions and the one based on planetary association/connection/dependence which eventually makes radical changes in Jupiter/Saturn's impact on the 8th house.

Planetary transit: -

If a transiting Planet finds some other planet in the sign of transit or the asterism (star) of its transit, the results will be good.

If a transiting planet finds no planets in the sign of transit or the asterism (star) and its group of anujanma, thirijanma stars – e.g. Aswini, Magam, Moolam – the results will not be good/appreciable.

Transit of Jupiter over natal (birth) Moon: -

This refers to the transit of a spiritual planet over the one ruling the mind and infusing spirituality. The aspect of Jupiter gives good results w rather than its conjunction/association. The conjunction of Jupiter with the Moon in the first house is not considered as good as it causes humiliation, shame, dejection or depression. Change of places and expensive travel are imminent. Invincible enemies form the attitude of household women.

While the difficult situations about Jupiter + Moon combinations are discussed, the question about the fortunes caused by the conjunction emerges. The answer is the conjunction of Jupiter + Moon confers basic amenities like food and clothing will be abundant but with some humiliation attached to it.

If this Jupiter + Moon combination presents in the 7th bhava of a native, it brings shame and humiliation through spouse/life partner or already adopted with humiliation. The native faces disastrous consequences based on the sign significators in which this combination is present.

The transit of Jupiter over the Moon posited in the asterisms (stars) of Jupiter or the Moon herself (Rohini, Hastha, Sravana) causes shame and disgrace which cannot be revealed/exposed.

A native had Moon in Poorva-Bhadra asterism (star). He got married in March and his mother had her second marriage in June within a gap of three months. The son got disgusted over the marriage of his mother and attempted to commit suicide as both mother and the son got married to members of the same family. Here, the Moon represents the body, mind, and mother of the native.

Example: -

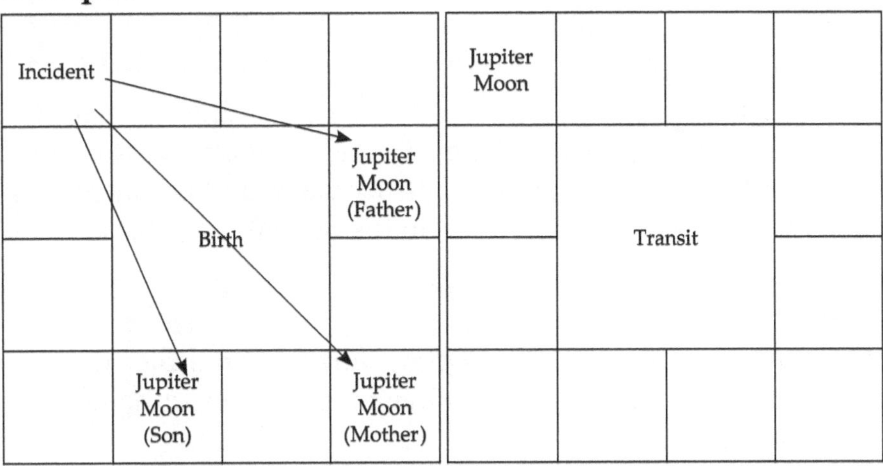

The above-displayed natal (birth) chart is that of a traditional heritage family.

In this, the father has Jupiter + Moon combination in Cancer, the mother in Virgo, and the son in Scorpio. Jupiter is traversing with Moon in Pisces. The son who was studying medicine absconded in a mentally retarded condition.

The planetary combination in a natal (birth) chart exhibits the results only when the same planetary combination takes place in transit.

Example: -

		Ketu					
	Birth	Jupiter Sun			Transit		
	Moon 2° Rahu 4°				Jupiter 3°		

In the above natal chart of a female, a debilitated Moon is afflicted by Rahu in Scorpio. She was severely infected by cancer in the uterus during the transit of Jupiter over her natal (birth) Moon.

The Moon in Scorpio badly affects the health of women. The lady faced severe physical disorders and ardent pain during the transit of Jupiter over her natal (birth) Moon and became worse as Rahu is associated with Moon in the natal (birth) chart.

Notes: –

While a powerful Moon gives good fortune, an afflicted Moon extends evil results and causes blemish or exposes hereditary/ancestral blemish.

This transit of Jupiter does affect women more than men. The impact of Jupiter on the afflicted Moon in conjunction with malefic, inimical planets will be more than the Moon who is alone in a sign. Jupiter's aspect gives good results than its presence in a sign. For Jupiter to extend better benefic results or less maleic results, he should be posited in the signs owned by the lords of lust (lords of 3rd/Mercury, 7th/Venus, and 11th/Saturn) to *Kalapurusha* (Time personified).

Transit of Jupiter over natal (birth) Mars: –

This transit refers to the planet representing fat over the indicator of blood, insisting on the need of arresting the cholesterol level in the body. As both Mars and Jupiter are the lords of the trines between them, a planned execution during their transit will produce the best results.

As Mars denotes house property and Jupiter to money, house construction can be undertaken during this transit. Jupiter being 'Dhanakaraka' or facilitator of money, this transit support construction of the house without any hassle.

This transit signifies the travel of an auspicious, benefic planet over the Kalathra karaka Mars clearing the path of marriage hurdles and supporting eligible groom and bride to get married.

Those who are suffering from blood-related diseases like low and high blood pressure should exercise caution during transit. This transit activates problems related to blood cholesterol and fatty tumours.

Transit of Jupiter over natal (birth) Mercury: -

1. The native will go in search of good friends.
2. Children will concentrate on their studies and will score good marks with merit.
3. As it is a transit of an indicator of affinity over a pointer of love, lovers will be very affectionate.
   Lovers should not have afflicted Mercury or Jupiter in their natal (birth) chart as this will result in pregnancy before marriage through love affairs.
4. Vacant land will fetch a good price. Unafflicted Mercury without the influence/association of Rahu will support income through vacant land.
5. Bank employees, typists, astrologers, and journalists/writers will get fame.
6. It will be a favourable time to get Bank loans.
7. Public speakers of any campaign with the Mercury + Ketu combination in their natal chart will receive good rewards and positions.

Transit of Jupiter over natal (birth) Jupiter: -

Jupiter will confer benefits to the native through its aspect or associations with other planets.

The aspect of Jupiter in transit to natal (birth) Jupiter: -

In the below natal (birth) chart, the ascendant lord of Mars is in cancer receiving the 9th aspect of Jupiter in Scorpio.

Example: –

	Ascendant					Jupiter	
		Mars					
	Birth				Transit		
Jupiter							

The native became more courageous than earlier during the transit of Jupiter in Taurus and his poor study in education improved making him get higher marks.

Though the ascendant lord Mars receives the aspect of Karaka for higher studies 9th lord Jupiter in the natal (birth) chart, gained strength during the transit period to bestow good results.

As Jupiter was posited in the 8th house to the ascendant and Mars in the 9th sign of affliction to the fixed sign Scorpio where Jupiter was positioned, the natal Jupiter's power was comparatively less to support education. But the transit of Jupiter in Taurus threw its aspect on natal Jupiter and energised it. The **aspect** of transit Jupiter is more powerful than its travel **over** natal Jupiter.

The results/benefits can be felt by the native only if transit Jupiter finds some planet in the sign of its transit. The results will be beneficial if the planets in the sign are benefic and it is otherwise in the case of malefic planets.

The absence of planets in the sign of transit and the debilitation of the lords of the asterism in which the transit of Jupiter occurs will render the results useless even though Jupiter is traversing over beneficial/powerful bhava.

Example: -

Birth

	Birth		Mars
		Sun	Ascendant

Transit

		Jupiter Ketu	
	Transit		
	Rahu		

For Virgo ascendant, Jupiter is traversing in a good position. During the transit of Jupiter in Kritika asterism (star), the star lord Sun was in debilitation in Libra forcing Jupiter to confer fewer benefits.

During the transit of Jupiter in the Rohini star, Ketu the obstructor conjoined Jupiter and prohibited big results to the native.

Along similar lines, the transit of Jupiter in Mrigasira star, the lord of the star Mars was in debilitation in Cancer allowing the native to enjoy only limited benefits.

For a transit Planet to extend its complete benefits the planet travelling along with it (planet posited in the same sign of transit) should also be a benefic and well-placed one. In addition to this, the lord of the asterism in which the transiting planet is moving and the sign lord of its transit should be in a good position as all three can be weighed at 33% each.

In this case, the lord of the asterism in which Jupiter travels carries 33% marks, the lord of the sign in which Jupiter passes over scores 33% marks and another 33% marks to a benefic planet travelling alongside Jupiter (only 10% in case the travelling planet is malefic).

Even though Ketu inflicts death during its association with other planets, it keeps a low profile like giving pain and problems instead of death or a painful death when associated with Jupiter. In total, Jupiter gives good results during its transit. **An unafflicted transit Jupiter confers basic facilities to the native for sure.**

Transit of Jupiter over natal (birth) Venus: -

It is like a worry-free journey in a luxury vehicle and also that of a Karaka for money (*dhanakaraka*) over the lord of the 2nd *(dhan sthan)* to *Kalapurusha* (Time personified). The significance of money is based on the combination/association of other planets giving economical comforts to these two planets.

A male with this sequence will be inclined to seek the love/company of a woman.

The native will be driven towards luxury enjoying a golden period of life. Jupiter and Venus though inimical against each other, will not oppose when the native likes the karaka of Venus. The native will go in search of luxurious, cosy places.

The women who are hitherto denied their husband's love, affection, and support will receive it during this transit period with a return of harmony in the family.

Greedy women will be netted in the bad company which will bring a bad name after the transit of Jupiter to the next sign insisting on being devoid of greed.

Ketu associated with Venus in the natal (birth) chart denies/makes us deny all benefits conferred by transit Jupiter over natal Venus.

An astrologer should assess and reveal the duration of the benefits that will be conferred by a planet.

Venus			Ketu
	Birth		Mars
	Example 1		
Rahu			

Venus	Ketu		
	Birth		
	Example 2		
		Rahu	

Example 1: –

During the transit of Jupiter over exalted Venus in Pisces, the native enjoyed all sorts of comforts and peace in family life. His wife was very affectionate to him.

Example 2: –

In this native (birth) chart, Ketu is posited in the sign next to Venus indicating its next transit over Venus. In this case, the native could not enjoy the comforts conferred by the transit of Jupiter over natal (birth) Venus even for a few months and as soon as Jupiter passed over to the next sign where Ketu is posited, he faced all sorts of crises and lost affinity towards his wife. The astrologer should reckon the transitory effects of the yearly planet Jupiter over benefic/malefic planets and accordingly reveal the duration/ continuance of the benefits conferred to the native until and after the transit.

A woman had a similar combination of example 2 chart in her native (birth) chart, Ketu in the next sign to Venus. She was in love which went on well until the transit of Jupiter over natal Venus once it passed on to the next sign where Ketu is, her love broke up and they are in separated for the past 3 years.

To get fruitful benefits during the transit, the transiting planet should find a friendlier planet in the next sign which is proved right in this natal chart.

Transit of Jupiter in Pisces over conjoined planets: -

<table>
<tr><td>Venus 16°
Saturn 10°</td><td></td><td></td><td>Saturn 16°
Venus 10°</td><td></td><td></td></tr>
<tr><td rowspan="2"></td><td rowspan="2">Birth
Example 1</td><td></td><td rowspan="2">Birth
Example 2</td><td></td><td rowspan="2"></td></tr>
<tr><td></td><td></td></tr>
<tr><td></td><td></td><td></td><td></td><td></td><td></td></tr>
</table>

In the above given two natal (birth) charts, there are two planets which will receive transit benefits from Jupiter and confer to the native. The karaka benefits based on their proximity to transiting Jupiter based on degree wise should be declared. Here, exalted Venus the karaka for women and affection, has conjoined the karaka for profession/business accounting for income.

Example 1: –

In the above chart, there are two planets conjoined and both derive benefit from transit Jupiter and convey it to the native. In this, Saturn is close to Jupiter degree-wise indicating the hardworking ability of the native bringing good profit in business which he invested in land, buildings, house properties, and vehicles, improving the status.

In Example 2, both conjoined Saturn and Venus transfer the benefit received from transit Jupiter to the native. In this case, Venus is close to Jupiter degree-wise indicating that the native received money earlier and did business with it and prospered. The money has come through their wife for investment in the business, as his efforts and hard work needed support. There will be a minor hitch like in this case of fortune derivative.

Analysis of the conjoined planets degree-wise will facilitate easy predictions which will be special and clear.

Associated planets confer their benefits according to their friendlier, inimical nature amongst them and their proximity to their degree of placement will determine the nature of the conferment of benefits.

Venus + Saturn combination/association confer good comforts during Jupiter's transit. Why?

Taurus Fortune		Venus	
	Example 3		
		Venus Sagittarius Fortune	

Saturn	Example 4		
Saturn Pisces Fortune			
Aquarius Fortune			

Kalapurusha (Time personified) philosophy answers the above question.

Libra sign owned by Venus is the house of fortune – the 11th house to the house of Jupiter- Sagittarius. On the reverse, the Pisces sign owned by Jupiter is the house of fortune – the 11th house to the house of Venus – Taurus.

Sagittarius sign owned by Jupiter is the house of fortune – the 11th house to the house of Saturn – Aquarius. On the reverse, the Capricorn sign owned by Saturn is the house of fortune – the 11th house to the house of Jupiter – Pisces.

Both Saturn and Venus are positioned in the 11th house of fortune either to or from Jupiter as per Kalapurusha (Time personified) philosophy, their conjunction or aspect brings fortune planetary-wise.

Between Saturn and Venus,

1. For Capricorn Saturn – Taurus Venus in trines (9) and Libra Venus in Kendra (10) (quadrants)
2. For Aquarius Saturn – Taurus Venus in quadrants (4) and Libra Venus in trines (9)

As both Saturn and Venus are friendlier amongst themselves, they do not compete in receiving the benefits from Jupiter and distributing them to the native.

The placement of other planets and the Maha Dasha (Dasha), and Antar Dasha (Bukthi) should support in retention of the benefits received through transit.

Transit of Jupiter over natal (birth) Saturn: -

This is the transit of an augmenter over the indicator of livelihood. Like the sweetening of bitter honey to taste by saliva, the transiting Jupiter transforms the fear about Saturn into a chill, sweet, and happy occasion.

It refers to the union of two of the yearly planets making significant changes in the lifestyle style/structure of a native. As indicators of karmic and, dharma (Righteousness) their union and transit will not harm.

This transit helps the native to lead a comfortable life. Even If Saturn and Jupiter are the evil lords as lords of the 8th, 6th, or death inflictor, the death during the transit will impart respect.

Those who like sour taste during this period and eat more of it will suffer diseases relating to sour taste.

This transit indicates the transit of a wage's payer Jupiter over that of labour working for wages indicated by Saturn which means proper payment for the work done. The beneficial positions of Jupiter and Saturn propel the native to get better placement and remuneration above his eligibility. **Transit of Jupiter over the 9th and 10th lords who are the dharma (Righteousness) and Karma lords respectively to the ascendant will also produce good results.**

The beneficial aspect of Jupiter on Saturn: -

The aspect of debilitated transit Jupiter over natal (birth) Saturn: -

Those with positions in their natal (birth) chart will comparatively less remuneration for the work they perform and will feel depressed through the work which will go waste. The anticipated income for the work done will not be there as per the proverb 'other side seems better than this side'. The native should talk more to go up the ladder.

The aspect of exalted Jupiter in transit over natal (birth) Saturn: -

The work done will be exemplary and fetch higher income with mental satisfaction and the association of respectable people. The transit Jupiter will meet natal (birth) Saturn once in 12 years.

The transit of Jupiter in trine to natal (birth) Saturn: -

The native will earn a good income in profession/business.

Transit of Jupiter in a Quadrant (Kendra/angle) to natal (birth) Saturn: -

The native will work to perfection but will receive no due income. Those who work for the welfare of the family but receive no recognition are born under this category, but their later life will be prosperous.

Had the placement of Saturn being in the houses of Jupiter – Sagittarius, Pisces – or in the asterisms (stars) of Jupiter Punarvasu, Visaka, Purva-Bhadra, the results will be extraordinary and will be ordinary otherwise. Such of those who have this placement in their natal (birth) chart, will see supreme results when their grandchildren attain 12 years of age and they will revive from their difficulties and will scale high from an ordinary level.

Transit of Jupiter in 3, 11 position to natal (birth) Saturn: -

The native will earn a good income in his profession/business and gets all his desires/wishes fulfilled through it.

Rahu/Ketu posited in the next sign to natal (birth) Saturn: -

The native who has Rahu/Ketu posited in the next sign to his natal (birth) Saturn has to struggle in his profession/business/job and face hindrances/crises.

The benefits bestowed by transit Jupiter will not last long and any abnormal results that are given will remain temporary but impact afterwards.

Example: –

	Birth		
	Saturn (Anuradha)		

Jupiter (Uthra-Bhadra)	Mars		
	Transit		
	Venus (Anuradha)		

Jupiter during its transit in Pisces throws its 9th aspect on natal (birth) Saturn posited in its star (asterism) Anuradha and helps those who have done the karaka businesses of Saturn and consultants/advisors to succeed to a great extent.

The transit chart can be observed to have two transits, 1) Venus's transiting in Saturn's Anuradha star and 2) Jupiter in Pisces in Saturn's Uthra-Bhadrada star and throwing its 9th aspect on Saturn as well. Thus, Saturn has gained double the strength of the benefic association of Venus and the aspect of Jupiter. The native got 60 lakhs of valued ancestral property through a lawsuit.

The transit occurred during the currency of Jupiter Maha Dasha (Dasha), Venus Antar Dasha (Bukthi), Saturn PrithyAntar Dasha (Anthram), Mars sookshma (sutchumam) involving three transits of Jupiter, Venus and Mars along with the aspect and star positions in the conferment of the results.

While arriving at the predictions, the planetary positions of all concerned should be taken into account as there may be multiple transits in operation simultaneously shedding different results.

Example: –

	Saturn (Barani)				Saturn (Barani)		
	Birth Person 1				Birth Person 2		
		Jupiter Venus			Jupiter Venus		

In the above natal chart of person 1, Saturn is posited in the Barani star owned by Venus. The native bought a house worth Rupees 75 lakh during the transit of Jupiter in Aries. This was possible without any obstacles due to the aspect received by Saturn from Jupiter who has conjoined Venus, the star lord of Barani where Saturn is posited.

The native of chart 2 was born a few days after person 1 who did not get a chance to build a house as he was running Rahu

Maha Dasha (Dasha). But from the first day of Jupiter's transit over natal (birth) Saturn, his problems got reduced and he got a noble spiritual Guru/preceptor/Guide. Gradually his income increased.

Person 1: –

As he was already in a wealthy status, he improvised his comforts.

Person 2: –

This person was already in the doldrums/debt, he could just recover from his debt and lead an ordinary life.

Both persons are fortunate to enjoy the benefits during the transit of Jupiter.

Transit of Jupiter over natal (birth) Rahu: –

It is the travel of a scarecrow over an insect that bites and a devout planet over the one that makes to frown. That of a benefic yearly planet over a malefic yearly planet gives far reaching-results which shackle the life of an individual.

A native with spiritual strength will glorify others and suffer without spiritual strength.

During the transit, the native will be pulled towards problems and will have the bad company of the mischievous.

The closeness of Jupiter and Rahu in transit will give serious troubles to the native when Rahu conjoins Jupiter or is posited in the next sign to Jupiter or close degrees in the natal chart.

1. The native will suffer chronic diseases forcing surgery.
2. The economic conditions of the natives will be a question mark.
3. In the case of children, they will face difficulties/dangers.
4. Progeny will be denied.
5. Treatment for artificial insemination has to be attempted by those who would like to beget children.

This is an ideal period to beget children the artificial means rather than any other time.

If the natives visit/pray/darshan the holy places/tombs of the mystics, they will be fully saved from all problems.

Transit of Jupiter over natal (birth) Ketu: -

This is the transit of a planet of virtues that drives towards salvation and gives wisdom. The native can gain spiritual strength. As one yearly planet is passing over another yearly planet, the benefits given by this transit will remain for a longer period and shackle the life of an individual.

1. The native will go in search of spiritual knowledge.
2. It is a period to seek legal remedies or compromise through an assembly of elders.
3. If Jupiter and Ketu are conjoined in the natal (birth) chart, this transit will lead to perversive arguments and an emptiness.
4. Those who are born during this transit will have Solomon's ring on their (Jupiter) finger which points them as an innovator.
5. The native will move from the devotional path to the spiritual path.

The close presence of Jupiter and Ketu in the natal (birth) chart: -

Had Jupiter and Ketu be closely associated in the natal (birth) chart and as well in transit with Maha Dasha (Dasha), Antar Dasha (Bukthi) of Jupiter, Ketu currently in operation, the problems posed by them will be at 100% level.

Note: -

If in a natal (birth) chart, two planets are either combined or in adjacent signs, a similar position during transit will cause 75% of problems which will escalate to 100% during the currency of the Maha Dasha (Dasha), Antar Dasha (Bukthi) of the same two planets.

Jupiter and Ketu in the natal (birth) chart and Transit: -

	Jupiter 9° Ketu 20°				Jupi- ter20° Ketu 5°	
	Birth 19.07.1976 21.55			Transit Surgery		

Date of Birth: 19.07.1976 – 21.55   Surgery for Cancer: 05.2012

Currently running Saturn Maha Dasha (Dasha) Jupiter Antar Dasha (Bukthi) Mercury PrithyAntar Dasha (Anthram).

In the above natal (birth) chart, Jupiter is posited in fewer degrees and Ketu in higher degrees indicating that Jupiter is afflicted by Ketu. During the transit, Ketu is present in fewer degrees and Jupiter in higher degrees in Taurus. The problems started when transit Ketu was in close degrees to natal Jupiter and aggravated when transit Jupiter closed in degree-wise to natal Ketu.

Here, transit Ketu has not exposed the disease as it was not connected as Maha Dasha (Dasha), Antar Dasha (Bukthi), PrithyAntar Dasha (Anthram) lord, but Jupiter as Antar Dasha (Bukthi) lord aggravated and exposed the problem.

Jupiter and Ketu are very close in degrees in the natal (birth) chart and their similar close position during transit caused the problem.

17.

VENUS IN TRANSIT

Lord Sukra (Venus) Gayathri:
Ohm aswathvajaya vidhmahe
Thanu hasthaya deemahi
Thanno Sukrah prachodayath

Let Lord Venus bestow his blessings on us to understand all his Karaka, bhava, and transit results

Transit Results: –
With the transit of Venus over its friendlier planets, the Karaka relations of Venus will be meritorious and will be impacted while moving over inimical planets.

18

KARAKATHUVAS OF VENUS

Venus in General: -

Karaka for women, Karaka for kalathra (spouse), lord of money, decoration/adornment, luxury, karaka for wife in case of a male, the character of the wife, indicator of past life karma through wife for husband and husband through wife. When Venus becomes 'dull' or moves close to the Sun, the fortune through their wife will not be there. It is virtuous to have Sukra not retrograde or 'dull' (moving close to the Sun) or associate/conjoin Rahu/Ketu in the natal (birth) chart.

Venus in relations: -

Aunt, elder sister, mother's elder/younger sister (Venus when associated or aspected by Saturn denotes younger sister and Venus associated or aspected by Moon denotes elder sister).

Venus in parts of the body: -

All glands, and secretive parts.

Venus in places: -

Venus specifies Luxurious and grandeur, lovable, beautiful, exotic places.

Venus in God/worship:

Meritorious/Virtuous and implicitly followed grandeur/ornamented Goddess as per Vedas. She is identified to depict the posture of Lord Vishnu when Venus is associated with Mercury and Lord Shiva when associated with Saturn + Sun.

Venus in business: -

Flower business, scented products, sale of products used by/related to women, silk thread, silk garments, jari works, textiles, fancy dress, ornaments, fancy products, sculptures, drawing, poets, music, percussionists, drama artists, folk artists, acting, players of music instruments, silver products, diamond, cat's eye, Gems, Cot, bed, pillow, furniture, liquor and alcoholic products, energy drinks, wholesale products, lust enhancers, logistics, sexual wellness products, business involving ladies, prostitutions, animal husbandry and business of animals, employment in aeroplanes like pilots/air hostess/technicians.

Transit of Venus: -

Venus takes 3 days and 8 hours to pass over one part of an asterism (star) moving at a speed of 1° 36′ 08″ a day. She retrogrades for one and half a month in 18 months of its rotation, taking approximately a month to pass over a sign and one year to move around the zodiac. The benefits good or bad extended by Venus will be more during the currency of the Maha Dasha (Dasha), Antar Dasha (Bukthi), and PrithyAntar Dasha (Anthram) of Venus and less when it is not. The native will not be devoid of good results and may suffer less inimical results.

Transit of Venus over natal (birth) Sun: -

1. As this is the transit of Karaka for money - Venus over karaka for father – Sun, the father of the native will see an elevation in his financial status and will receive outstanding money.
2. Assuming the Sun is an administrator/Manager of the form owned by the native, the administrator/Manager will be inclined towards luxury or women. Hence caution should be exercised to see that there is no interference by women in administration. Even helping them will result in a bad name.
3. The native's father will be approached by his sisters for any financial favours or property.

4. Eyes should be checked as they may get affected. Cataract formation and eye discharge are the probable diseases.
5. Venus helps in locating the possible good and bad results to the father, eldest son, elder sister of the father, administrators/ Managers.
6. For a possible transformation of change in attitude to an event, the combined Maha Dasha (Dasha), Antar Dasha (Bukthi), and PrithyAntar Dasha (Anthram) of the Sun and Venus should be in operation.
7. This may even be the Maha Dasha (Dasha), Antar Dasha (Bukthi), or PrithyAntar Dasha (Anthram) of the planets either in the signs belonging to the Sun, Venus or their asterisms (stars).

Transit of Venus over natal (birth) Moon: -

1. Desires and love will voluntarily attract the native.
2. Daughters-in-law will be engaged in quarrels and scuffle voluntarily with mother -n-law.
3. Young girls will voluntarily approach elderly women and cause hatred.
4. There will be a deficiency in glands and secretive parts of the body.

Transit of Venus over natal (birth) Mars: -

1. Women will seek friendship voluntarily.
2. Sisters who parted ways will unite together.
3. Vehicle owners will remodel/redesign them.
4. Money against the house, and land will be available.

In the case of women: -

1. Ladies will volunteer in seeking the friendship of gents. Married women will unite with husbands who were in separation and will become pregnant.
2. Vehicle owners will remodel/redesign them.

Transit of Venus over natal (birth) Mercury: -

Mercury is responsible for mischief in marital relations and drives towards extra-marital relations. It will cause problems in newly married relations.

In the case of women: -

They will go in search of their beau and poke their nose in their family life. They will get separated had this been a bad Maha Dasha (Dasha), Antar Dasha (Bukthi).

In the case of Men: -

In the case of married men, their wives will cause havoc in family life instigating events of a previous love affair and leading to separation in family life and between the couple making it worse in case of a malefic Maha Dasha (Dasha), Antar Dasha (Bukthi).

Example: -

Venus 9°		Ketu				Ketu	
	Birth				Transit		
Mars Rahu		Ascendant			Venus Rahu		

The above natal (birth) chart of Virgo ascendant has exalted Venus in Pisces in trines to Mars conjoined Rahu in Scorpio.

Venus is associated with Rahu during her transit in Scorpio. On the third day of Venus's entry in Scorpio, problems erupted between husband and wife leading to the extent of seeking a legal separation. The wife went in search of her husband who has gone to visit his parents and saw him in an uncompromisable position and quarrelled with him.

In this natal chart, Mars occupies his own house indicating that the husband is in his own house and association of Mars, Rahu – to his uncompromisable position. Transit of Venus in Scorpio – a house owned by Mars – indicates the wife's visit to the husband's house to find him indulging in wrong activities.

Had Mars been posited alone in this chart (without Rahu in the natal chart), he would have bestowed good fortunes and his association with Rahu conveyed malefic results. There are two transits in the operation of which Rahu has not influenced any problems through their wife even months after its entry emphasising the transit of Venus as the sole cause for the problems.

Transit of Venus over natal (birth) Jupiter: -

This refers to the transit of two auspicious planets, monthly Venus over yearly Jupiter conferring 75% of beneficial results and not fearful events.

It can be compared to a person with a small means meeting an aristocrat and to that of an event giving joy to one and sorrow to another by the influence of the transit of Venus.

For Example: -

A girl eloped with her beau and got married, which brought joy to her but caused sorrow to her parents who do not support her love which indicates the two sides of good and bad resultants of Venus transit.

This transit hurts progeny based on significators of the ascendant pointing at problems in glands.

Example: –

<table>
<tr><td>Ketu</td><td>Jupiter 13°
Venus 22°</td><td></td><td></td></tr>
<tr><td rowspan="2"></td><td colspan="2" rowspan="2">Birth</td><td></td></tr>
<tr><td></td></tr>
<tr><td>Ascen-
dant</td><td></td><td>Rahu</td><td></td></tr>
</table>

<table>
<tr><td></td><td>Venus 9°
Jupiter 22°</td><td></td><td></td></tr>
<tr><td rowspan="2"></td><td colspan="2" rowspan="2">Transit</td><td></td></tr>
<tr><td></td></tr>
<tr><td></td><td></td><td></td><td></td></tr>
</table>

The above lady is born in Sagittarius ascendant having lords of the 4th Jupiter and 6th Venus in the 5th house, an indicator of progeny. She was running the Maha Dasha (Dasha), and Antar Dasha (Bukthi) of Venus during its transit in Aries causing health issues reckoned as thyroid from tests conducted. She was told that her health will improve only when her thyroid level is brought under control.

The natal Venus is in 22.29° and Jupiter is in 13.29°

The transit Venus is in 9.00° and the transit Jupiter in 22.21°

Venus is transiting over natal Jupiter and Jupiter is traversing over natal Venus. Thyroid problem affects conception. But the native had financial gains.

Jupiter is posited in Ketu's asterism in the natal chart and Ketu is placed in the 12th sign Pisces to Jupiter and Venus in Aries in the natal chart. Transit Jupiter and Venus should pass over natal Ketu before entering into Aries where their embryonic capabilities are affected. As they are close to natal Jupiter and Venus, they affected childbirth.

Note: -

If benefic planets have to cross over malefic planets in transit before approaching another benefic, their planetary life strength or their moral strengths are seriously affected.

This equally holds good when the transiting planets are to cross the planets in which the natal planets are posited and their star lords are stationed.

Transit of Venus over natal (birth) Venus: -

This is the transit of a monthly planet. The native **could not** enjoy any beneficial results **if Venus is alone** in the natal chart or **not that of Maha Dasha (Dasha), Antar Dasha (Bukthi), and Prityantar Dasha (Anthram) of Venus. The association of Venus and Jupiter in the natal chart assure receipt of anticipated money during the transit.**

Transit of Venus over natal (birth) Saturn: -

It is a transit of a monthly planet over its friendlier yearly planet extending very beneficial results. As both Venus and Saturn are evil mongers and death inflictors for the Aries ascendant, their transit will cause lethal incidents and even death at times.

1. The native will face monetary problems at his workplace. The money due will be received after struggles. There will be rightful compensation for the labour put in. The combination of Saturn and Venus in transit over the combined Saturn and Venus natal chart has driven the natives to lose their life of excess greed to make quick money.
   Abnormal improbable quoted by a few who wanted to make big money is as follows:
   a) Making Viagra from Deer antlers.
   b) Electricity from Water
   c) Using neem stems as mobile phones for communication
   Greedy people lost their savings, income, and future.
2. Distress and difficulties will be through unknown ladies.

3. Care should be exercised while dealing with servants, and siblings of parents. Their spendthrift nature will cause a financial burden to the natives as will be indicated by this transit.

Transit of Venus over natal (birth) Rahu: -

This is the transit of a monthly planet over a malefic yearly planet. The karaka relations denoted by Venus will be driven towards illegal actions and illicit relationships. Ladies will get their wishes fulfilled which may seem to be good but not for real.

The native will find problems in the workplace because of money or through unknown ladies. It will induce to offer or receive a bribe to get a thing done and it will lead to mystery during unfavourable Maha Dasha (Dasha), Antar Dasha (Bukthi). The job will not be done unless money is spent.

It will be a good period for cine workers, photo/video studios, and drama artists.

The native will seek bad company and will invite problems.

Problems, litigations, and legal issues will arise during the attempts to demand money lent.

A few may obviate/leave/relocate their homeland in distress while some others will live in exile/prison. Many people were cheated or getting cheated to the extent that they can never come up in their life.

As Rahu induces greed in a person, many people have lost their lives by being greedy. (Rahu is responsible for greed).

This transit may see some people in prison or living in absconding/hiding. (This will be known as prison time).

This transit pushes a native towards excessive desires and attempts any means to get their wishes fulfilled.

Transit of Venus over natal (birth) Ketu: -

This is a transit of an auspicious monthly planet over a yearly planet that cause separation.

Ketu represents law, rules and regulations. During the transit of Venus over Ketu, the bhava in which Venus travels has the karaka of Venus namely litigation, separation, loneliness, and vacuum will be experienced. Even smaller mistakes will cause great problems. Those who are already facing family problems will face more litigation and legal issues through women.

Married persons who have bitter relationships with their spouses may look for separation through legal means failing which the problems will escalate. The problems will end all of a sudden.

Legal issues in ancestral properties will arise and property claims with sisters; will escalate leading to looking for legal remedies.

In the absence of legal complications with sisters', wives or any other woman whom the native is fond of will create problems. This transit period may cause death to some ladies in the family.

Rather than Ketu in a lonely placement, his association with any other planets like Mandi (Gulikan), Saturn, Venus, Moon, or Mars and the transit of Venus over these combined planets aggravates the problems and had this be the Maha Dasha (Dasha), Antar Dasha (Bukthi), or PrithyAntar Dasha (Anthram) of Venus the lethal events or even death may be caused.

While Ketu denotes separation and problems, Venus points to happiness and luxury. Hence the transit of these two contrasting planets will confer only contrasting results pardoning those with limited desires but punishing greedy people.

Venus and Ketu in worship: –

Worship of Lord Ganesh when Venus is ruling and exalted.

Worship of Lord Nandi (Bull) when associated with the Sun or in the Sun sign Leo.

Worship of ferocious Goddess Durga when associated with the Moon or in the Moon sign Cancer.

Worship of Goddess Prithyankara when associated with Mars or in Martian signs Aries/Scorpio.

Worship Lord Adhisesha (Serpent) when associated with Mercury or in Mercury signs Gemini/Virgo.

Worship of Preceptors/spiritual teachers, when associated with Jupiter or in Jupiter, signs Sagittarius/Pisces.

Adoption of Vrats by straining body like fasting, rolling in shrines, walking miles to temples, etc. when associated with Saturn or in Saturn signs Capricorn/Aquarius.

The above performances will reduce the impact/problems caused by the transit of Venus/Ketu.

When will the native realise/feel the impact of malediction?

The native will feel the presence of malediction/curse during the transit of Venus over natal (birth) Rahu/Ketu or transit of Rahu/Ketu over natal (birth) Venus.

What is the definition of malediction/Curse:

1. The Mother who is not affectionate.
2. The Father who has not imparted knowledge.
3. Preceptor who has not enhanced his disciple's knowledge.
4. The God which has not helped to resolve the problems.
5. Food that does not satisfy hunger.
6. Water that cannot quench the thirst.
7. The holy water that has not driven out the evil.
8. Wife who is not supportive.
9. Woman who is unknown to save.
10. Unaccommodating friend.
11. Non-exciting lover.
12. Unsupportive children in case of need.
13. Uncompromising friendship.
14. Unmindful of God's presence.

Ketu's lone position vs conjunction with a planet: -

<table>
<tr><td></td><td>Ketu</td><td></td><td></td><td>Mars 5°
Ketu 9°</td><td></td></tr>
<tr><td>Example 1</td><td></td><td></td><td>Example 2</td><td></td><td></td></tr>
<tr><td>Rahu</td><td></td><td></td><td>Rahu 9°</td><td></td><td></td></tr>
</table>

In both natal (birth) charts, Venus is transiting over Ketu in Taurus.

Example 1: -

Ketu is alone in Taurus, and Venus is passing over it. Here it gave no big impacts and no reason attributed to a minor impact felt.

Example 2: -

In this example, Ketu in Taurus is associated with Mars and both are malefic and inimical to each other.

The native of the above chart was driven by greed forcing him to buy land at a cheap price and got cheated an impact by Mars whose karaka played the role.

Mars unafflicted by Ketu gives the strength to bear the impact whereas it will be unbearable when Mars is afflicted by Ketu.

When Ketu is alone, the impact caused by the transit of a planet over it will not be exposed but it will be explicit when it is combined/associated with another planet during the transit of a planet over it.

19.

SATURN IN TRANSIT

Lord Shani (Saturn) Gayathri:

Ohm kakathvajaya vidhmahe

Katka hasthaya deemahi

Thanno manthah prachodayath

Let Lord Saturn bestow his blessings on us to understand all his Karaka, bhava, and transit results

Transit Results: –

With the transit of Saturn over its friendlier planets, the Karaka relations of Saturn will be meritorious and will be impacted while moving over inimical planets.

20.

KARAKATHUVAS OF SATURN

Saturn in General: -

Dull, old, dirty, laziness, heritage, antiquity, interest in antic products, actions/events causing worries. Saturn causes a delay in all actions and hence delays the results through the bhava in which it is posited. Saturn is responsible for the high and low life of a person.

Saturn in relations/persons: -

Younger male siblings of father, servants, labourers, subservient, inferior relations, priests/pundits who conduct marriages or ceremonial prayers.

Saturn in parts of the body: -

Legs, visible veins of the body, and parts where dirt deposits are seen.

Saturn in places: -

Dirty places and places where dirt is collected.

Saturn in God: -

Guardian deities like Karuppusamy, Ayyanar, Annamar, Karupparayar and Deities in open grounds without a roof above them.

Saturn in products/articles: -

Scrap, antics, heritage products, memorials, monuments, mementoes, dirty things, unorthodox products

Saturn in business/job: -

Coal business, Jailor, buying and selling barren land, tinning, less paid/menial jobs, begging, research, burial related jobs/morgue cutting, monks/saints, building construction jobs, agriculture, wretched life, pottery, tinware jobs, mining, porters, load man, rag picking, scavenger, candles, lacquer, livestock traders, cobblers, gardeners, coolies, iron, oil, cereal/nuts trading, jute and coir, gunny bags, remodelling/restructuring of old products, electrical work, building contract, repair work, painting, executioners, slavery, mustard, black gram/urad, sesame trade.

Saturn as Karma karaka: -

What is the Karma behind the association of two people? What is their ancestral birth relationship? What is the occupation of a person? All the above questions are answered by the position of Saturn. The means of Survival and food are the two senses of a person and when the natal (birth) Saturn is not well placed his occupation and food to eat will not be in order and so is his karma.

Transit of Saturn: -

As Saturn is a yearly planet, its transit effect will last long and as Saturn has too many inimical planets, the benefic results extended by it will be minimum. Even though the malediction of other planets is more, since being associated with them, Saturn is termed as the most malefic of all as beneficiaries of Saturn are very few.

Saturn takes approximately one month to pass over one degree and three months to cross over one part of an asterism (star), 30 months to move through one sign, and full 30 years to complete one cycle of the zodiac.

Rheumatism and Saturn: -

Rheumatism and neuro disorders are closely related to Saturn. The karaka relations indicated by the planet in association/ combination/conjunction of Saturn in the natal (birth) chart or transit will suffer rheumatism or neurological disorders.

Saturn during its transit over the natal (birth) Sun causes rheumatism and neurological disorders to any one of the fathers, father-in-law, eldest son, or managers of the firm/company owned by the native.

Saturn during its transit over the natal (birth) Moon causes rheumatism and neurological disorders to any one of the mothers, mother-in-law, or elderly women in the family.

Saturn during its transit over natal (birth) Mars causes rheumatism and neurological disorders to any one of brother, brother-in-law, or close blood relations.

Saturn during its transit over natal (birth) Mercury causes rheumatism and neurological disorders to any one uncle, close friend, or younger sister.

Saturn during its transit over natal (birth) Jupiter causes rheumatism and neurological disorders to any one of grandfathers, grandmothers, elderly persons, or children.

Saturn during its transit over natal (birth) Venus causes rheumatism and neurological disorders to any one of the aunts, siblings of the father or the mother.

Saturn during its transit over natal (birth) Saturn causes rheumatism and neurological disorders to any one of the grateful servants, younger siblings of the father, father-in-law, and temple priests.

Saturn during its transit over natal (birth) Rahu/Ketu causes rheumatism and neurological disorders to either grandfather or grandmother.

If the karaka relations are not affected, the native will be affected by rheumatism sort of ailments in the parts of the body marked by the karaka, like

Paraplegia or Arthritis of the hands and feet, paralysis, rheumatoid arthritis, cerebral palsy, bell's palsy, hemiplegia, and muscle cramps.

Transit of Saturn through 12 signs from the ascendant: -

Transit of Saturn in the ascendant: -

Causes depression/mental agony, laziness and pushes towards life in distant/unknown or below-par places.

Transit of Saturn in the 2nd house to ascendant: -

The native will face humiliation in the family. Depending upon the significators (Capricorn/Aquarius) of Saturn in the natal (birth) chart, any one of theft, love affairs, money matters or borrowings will bring an ever-lasting bad name to self or family.

Had Saturn been posited in the 2nd house or connected to the 2nd house, Saturn's movements relating to the above positions will cause unbearable humiliation and distress impacting the native to commit suicide.

The aspect of Saturn in transit to natal (birth) Saturn in the 2nd, 5th, 8th, or 12th house is sure to cause distress and shame and if this transit coincides with the death afflicting Maha Dasha (Dasha), Antar Dasha (Bukthi) will force the death of the native.

Transit of Saturn in the 3rd house to ascendant: -

The father of the native will have to relocate and the native will suffer blemish in progeny.

Transit of Saturn in the 4th house to ascendant: -

The native will suffer from diseases, diseases due to the deeds of the past (karmic origin), and face fateful deeds. Saturn will aspect the ascendant, 6th house and the 10th house from where it is posited extending the disease (impact of the 6th house) and Karmic events like performing death rituals (impact of the 10th house) to the native (ascendant) through the karaka of the planet posited in the transiting sign.

Transit of Saturn in the 5ᵗʰ house to ascendant: -

Saturn will impart sorrow through children and by affecting progeny due to blemish. Transit Saturn in the 5ᵗʰ house will throw its aspect on the 7ᵗʰ house (thro' 3ʳᵈ aspect), 11ᵗʰ house (thro' 7ᵗʰ aspect), and 2ⁿᵈ house (10ᵗʰ aspect) causing a delay in marriage and preventing marriage in some cases. The planets posited in the 2ⁿᵈ, 7ᵗʰ, and 11ᵗʰ houses will assist or be responsible for the action of Saturn in prevention or delay.

In my experience, I strongly reiterate that a planet/sign/bhava which receives the aspect of another planet is responsible for the delay of an event/action.

Transit of Saturn in the 6ᵗʰ house to ascendant: -

The chronic and serious disease causes death during this transit. The borrowing power of the native increases and any misuse of the borrowed funds results in severe punishment getting branded as a cheat.

Transit of Saturn in the 7ᵗʰ house to ascendant: -

Here, Saturn causes the blemish termed as *'Punarpoo'* – a hindrance in marriage. The marriage will be below par and receive criticism.

As Saturn attains 'Dig Bala' or directional strength, success will be achieved when attempting actions that were impossible earlier.

Transit of Saturn in the 8ᵗʰ house to ascendant: -

This transit causes humiliation after marriage but increases longevity.

Transit of Saturn in the 9ᵗʰ house to ascendant: -

There will be trouble for the native's father and the native if in management. In case this happens to be the death-inflicting period to the native's father, it may cause death to him. Both native's father and the native's administrative expenses will be pushed towards debt.

Transit of Saturn in the 10th house to ascendant: -

This is a period of performing karmic events like death rituals but enhances business prosperity and job opportunities.

Transit of Saturn in the 11th house to ascendant: -

The desires of the native will be fulfilled and will be a golden period. It will bring more prosperity if Jupiter or Venus is posited in the 11th house.

Transit of Saturn in the 12th house to ascendant: -

It will be a restless period with the impact of debt, humiliation or family squabbles.

All the above are only common results but are sure to take place. If the transiting planet finds another planet in its sign of transit, the combined results of Saturn's position concerning ascendant and combined planetary effects should be reckoned. Instead of reckoning the lone Saturn's transit results, the combined effects of natal (birth) Saturn in association with other planets which would have changed in transit should also be considered for evaluation and arriving at a final prediction.

Saturn in natal (birth) chart and its relativity with 'Pancha Pakshi' (Five Birds): -

Pancha Pakshi or Five Birds – as it is called – is an embodiment of five elements (Pancha Bhutas) of the earth helping to identify the active period to get good/favourable results.

The five acts/statuses of the 'Pancha Patchi' are:
- Sleeping
- Walking
- Eating

- Ruling
- Dead (Inactive)

1. Saturn conjoined/associated with Sun represents the sleeping stage.
2. Saturn conjoined/associated with Moon represent the walking state.
3. Saturn conjoined/associated with Jupiter represent in eating stage.
4. Saturn conjoined/associated with Venus represents the powerful ruling position.
5. Saturn conjoined/associated with Rahu/Ketu denotes half-death status.
6. Saturn conjoined/associated with Rahu/Ketu/Mandi denotes death status.

A planet will extend benefits in transit based on its association with the natal (birth) chart which is the reason for the variance in the results for different people.

For example, let us analyse the transit of Saturn: -

Let us assume that Saturn is associated with the Sun in the natal (birth) chart. In whichever sign Saturn move during transit, it will carry the character, swiftness, and significators of the Sun along with its karakathuvas.

Saturn associated with Moon in the natal (birth) chart will carry the character, swiftness and significators of the Moon along with its karakathuvas in whichever sign it goes in transit.

Saturn associated with Mars in the natal (birth) chart will carry the character, swift actions and significators of Mars along with its karakathuvas in whichever sign it goes in transit.

Saturn's transit impact in the sign where Saturn is associated with Rahu/Ketu will be very severe rather than over its lone position.

Saturn who is associated with an inimical planet in the natal (birth) chart will exhibit a severe impact when transiting in a sign where already an inimical planet is posited. The enmity between the planet aggravates as their inimical character is impacted.

On the contrary, the enmity level decreases when Saturn is associated with a friendlier planet in the natal (birth).

Saturn's transit in Libra sign for two persons running different Maha Dasha (Dasha), Antar Dasha (Bukthi): -

Person 1: -

During Saturn's transit in Libra, the native suffered a lot but did not run away from home town as he could bear the impact with a supportive Maha Dasha (Dasha) and Antar Dasha (Bukthi).

Person 2: -

In his case, Saturn's impact was unbearable to the extent that he has been forced to run away from his hometown as the Maha Dasha (Dasha), and Antar Dasha (Bukthi) in operation was not supportive. His creditors proceeded legally against him.

Transit of Saturn over natal (birth) Sun: -

It is a transit of a dark planet over a bright luminary and that of subordinates approaching the manager/administrator. Those in power/administration will face problems through their subordinates/workers. Servants will bother their employers.

The native will face diseases accrued due to past life/karmic effect indicating the passage of one part of the life.

The work burden of the father will increase. In the case of the son who is too affectionate with his father, his father will face health issues or death-like eventualities during the transit of Saturn over the Sun.

The same is the case with the father-in-law of the native.

For those who are in search of eternal wisdom and meditation, this transit is a perpetual period to move on the spiritual path to the spiritual light.

The native will face problems from Government authorities and jobs will see a setback.

Example: -

	Birth	Sun 14°.00″ Mars 14°20″		Transit	Saturn

In the above chart, the Sun is in Leo posited at 14° and the evil monger for the Fixed sign Leo, 9th lord Mars is posited in the same Leo sign at 14°20′ close to the Sun. The enmity is aggravated as Mars is inimical to the Sun.

When Saturn, who is inimical to both Mars and the Sun traversed over Leo, the native who travelled with his father-in-law in a two-wheeler met with an accident in which his father sustained severe injuries and the native too suffered injuries. The native's father too met with an accident. During Saturn's transit period of two and a half years, both accidents took place giving severe impacts.

Transit of Saturn over the sign in which Mars is posited confirms the occurrence of an accident and karaka'srelation involved in the accident will be identified by the planet posited along with Mars who is the Sun in this case.

Example: –

<table>
<tr><td colspan="3" rowspan="2"></td><td rowspan="2"></td><td colspan="3" rowspan="2"></td></tr>
<tr></tr>
<tr><td></td><td rowspan="2">Birth</td><td>Ascen-
dant</td><td></td><td rowspan="2">Transit</td><td></td></tr>
<tr><td></td><td>Sun
Venus</td><td></td><td>Saturn</td></tr>
<tr><td colspan="3"></td><td></td><td colspan="3"></td></tr>
</table>

In the above Cancer ascendant chart, the Sun and Venus are placed in the 2nd house and Saturn is transiting in Leo. Of the two native planets, beneficial Venus is supporting the visiting Saturn in the form of financial help from a bank and through the father.

Saturn denotes win disease rheumatism. During the transit of Saturn over the Sun, the native's father was suffering from rheumatism as Saturn imparted disease to the father as a friendlier planet of Venus than its enmity with the Sun. Instead, Saturn gave good results to the Sun apart from bad results.

The native was running Venus Maha Dasha (Dasha), and Antar Dasha (Bukthi) of the Sun, which is that of the lord of the disease 6th Leo, the Sun and lord of the evil 8th Libra, Venus considering Pisces as ascendant – an indicator of 9th house, father for Cancer ascendant.

Here, Venus is the lord of the evil 8th house to father turns out to be lord of the benefit as well affliction to the Sun with Cancer ascendant thus giving disease to the father and financial benefits to the Son.

Example: -

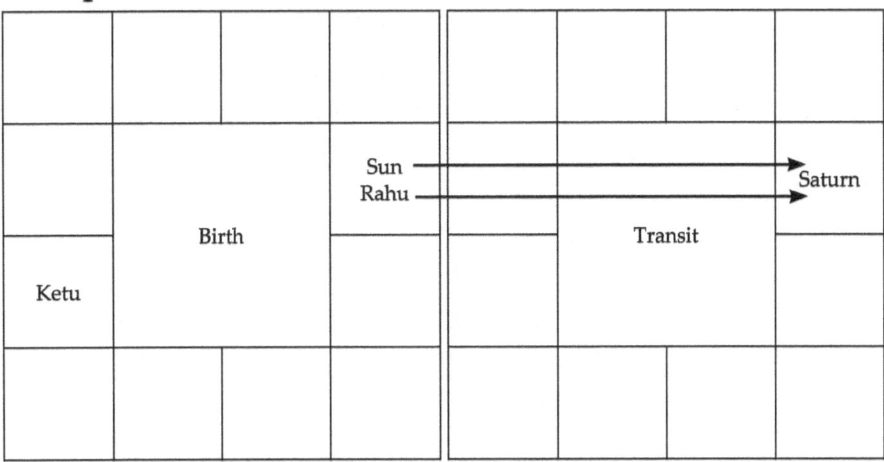

In the above natal chart, the Sun and Rahu are conjoined in Cancer and Saturn is moving into Cancer in transit. The native is already suffering in business administration due to the affliction of the Sun – an indicator of administration/management and Rahu towards financial problems. Saturn denotes small loans.

To revive the business administration and expand the business the native ventures for further loans. In the initial stages, it appeared to be set right but it did not and pushed the native into a huge debt that could not be repaid even after 5 long years. While Rahu induces greed to go for big, Ketu knits the web as those who got in could never get out.

For people with such entanglement, the impact may reduce or add depending upon the Maha Dasha (Dasha), and Antar Dasha (Bukthi) but will not be forbidden/stopped completely. During the transit period, the native got his father operated on for cataracts in the eyes.

The Sun is the karaka for eyes. As Rahu is with the Sun, it caused problems in eyes of the father (The Sun denotes father as well as eyes) during the entry of Saturn into Cancer.

Had this been a death-inflicting (Maraka) period Maha Dasha (Dasha), Antar Dasha (Bukthi) to the native's father, he would have died. As he is not running inimical Maha Dasha, Antar Dasha he has to suffer lethal problems.

Rahu is inimical to the Sun and their combination is so lethal and entry of Saturn, another inimical planet to both Rahu and the Sun aggravates the inimical feelings giving complications instead of good results.

Transit of Saturn over the Sun in Aries: -

This transit takes place in a sign where the Sun is exalted and Saturn is in a debilitated condition. Here Saturn will not harm the father in any big way and will give only minor problems.

Transit of Saturn over the Sun in Libra: -

Here, Saturn is exalted and the Sun is in debilitated condition inferring that the father will suffer big problems. He will not be bothered much by his son's problems.

Transit of Saturn over the Sun in the house of Venus – Taurus and Libra: -

The Sun receives the significators of Venus in Taurus and Libra depicting the supremacy of Venus in all events involving the father and the son which implicates the role of the karaka of Venus in all contradictions between the father and son or between a manager/administrator and his servants/subordinates.

Transit of Saturn over the Sun in Jyeshta asterism (star) of Mercury and posited in Scorpio: -

The father of the native will be a very stubborn and strict disciplinarian who will face his problems with much mental stress and stubbornness. He will be hateful towards his relations and expose his problems.

Transit of Saturn over the Sun in Chitta asterism (star) of Mars and posited in Virgo: -

The father will be intelligent, shrewd, keen in his job and handle income and expenditures prudently. He will smartly face problems during the transit of Saturn over the Sun, will not be hatred towards his relations and will not expose his problems.

The difference between the above two can be distinguished as that of Mercury's star in the ferocious Mars sign and the star of Mars in the calm Mercury sign.

Transit of Saturn over the Sun in Mrigasira asterism (star) of Mars and posited in Gemini: -

The natives will engage themselves in dance, drama, and music to get rid of their problems which increase, decrease or neutralise the problems. When discussing such diversions, they argue as great philosophers. In the Gemini sign, the Sun acts as the representative of Mercury by sharing his problems and in the Virgo sign, the Sun acts as the representative of Mercury but is not willing to share his problems and handle them by himself.

It should be noted that a planet will get a change in its character and actions but not in its karakathuvas due to the influence of the sign lord and star lord where it is posited.

Transit of Saturn over the natal (birth) Moon: -

This is the centre/mid-period of Sade-Sati an eventful Seven-and-a-half-year journey of Saturn over the natal (birth) Moon and its adjacent signs, considered a life-threatening period. The fear over this cannot be simply rubbed off but it is not that threatening for real.

It portrays health issues to the native or his mother or his mother-in-law living with him.

Real hard workers will gain through this period and reap a good harvest of benefits in this golden period. Their hard work will be helpful to others.

Those who try hard in their attempts will get good opportunities in business and jobs but not instantaneously. Every time the native will have to face tough situations and severe problems until he feels exhausted. This exertion is what people fear in general.

As Saturn is considered a Judge and evaluator of karmic results, he examines each individual before giving benefits and the difficulties imparted by him are always for good.

An action undertaken may be interrupted and stopped at any moment during this transit.

For example.,
1) Cancellation of a scheduled marriage
2) Inability to purchase or sell off land agreed.

Such obstructions in any event at any point in time can be felt through this transit.

Different results will be exhibited by the Moon which is along in a sign and conjunction with another planet.

Transit of Saturn over natal (birth) Moon posited alone: -

This is referred to in transit as 'Jenma Shani' specifying as 'at birth'. The native will be relocated, will be affected by diseases, will feel mental stress, and will do public service during this transit.

Transit of Saturn in the 2ⁿᵈ house to natal (birth) Moon: -

It is called the 3ʳᵈ leg of Sade-Sati or the end part of the seven-and-a-half-year period of Saturn in transit. The native's mind will always be thinking about the business or job engaged in but the opportunities and family environment will not support such attempts. There will be humiliation either to the native or the native's family through the native.

Transit of Saturn in the 3rd house to natal (birth) Moon: -

The native will have a restless mind in the business/job engaged in. Success will be assured when things are attempted without greed. Business ventures should be without the involvement of ladies in the case of male natives and without the involvement of gents in the case of female natives to avoid lousy remarks/awful names otherwise the business will have to be closed due to the failure of invigilance in each other's actions.

The transiting Saturn in the 3rd house should not find a debilitated Moon or Saturn conjoined with Rahu/Ketu to avoid facing unending problems.

Transit of Saturn in the 4th house to natal (birth) Moon: -

This transit is termed semi-evil. Persons having such type of situations will be interested in self-employment and will carefully attempt to attain it. They should not reveal their plans as they will not fructify when their plans are revealed. If they keep their plans a secret till execution, they will succeed during this transit.

Transit of Saturn in the 5th house to natal (birth) Moon: -

The native will get income to meet the expenses of children but not enough for self-expenses. It will be a period of humiliation and either the native will face insult or bring disrepute to his family.

Transit of Saturn in the 6th house to natal (birth) Moon: -

There are chances of unplanned business ventures failing. Job goers will find this transit period as good. Patients will suffer due to increased pain and resultant expenditures causing fear. There will be a humiliation to the native or native's family through the native.

Transit of Saturn in the 7th house to natal (birth) Moon: -

This is also considered an evil transit. Those with the aim of self-employment/individual business will not find favourable circumstances or opportunities leaving them and their family in the total lurch. During this period, the transit of Rahu/Ketu will determine the sudden loss of income.

Both fortunes and misfortunes will be in abundance and careful consideration of the transit of Rahu/Ketu will support new business proposals.

Transit of Saturn in the 8ᵗʰ house to natal (birth) Moon: -

This transit is referred to as an evil 8ᵗʰ house Saturn driving the native to anything indiscriminately in greed. There will be no relativity between a thought and its execution or any planning which may lead to failure in business. Had this been a period of Jupiter's transit over natal Jupiter, those in business will be responsible to close their business by themselves due to excessive greed as they will not be mentally strong.

Transit of Saturn in the 9ᵗʰ house to natal (birth) Moon: -

The native will meet the medical expenses of his father and if this happens to be the 'maraka' or death-inflicting Maha Dasha (Dasha), or Antar Dasha (Bukthi) period, he will meet with death.

Transit of Saturn in the 10ᵗʰ house to natal (birth) Moon: -

The native will fully understand his business during this transit which will help him to scale up in later life. This will be possible only when the Moon or Saturn is not afflicted by Rahu/Ketu. The native will have thought about business in his 10ᵗʰ, 27ᵗʰ, and 28ᵗʰ year of age. During this transit period, the native may incur medical expenses for his father/wife and the father may face death if this happens to be the death-inflicting Maha Dasha (Dasha), or Antar Dasha (Bukthi).

Transit of Saturn in the 11ᵗʰ house to natal (birth) Moon: -

The urge to do individual business will be haunting the native during this transit. There will be a mental struggle to do better business than in any other period.

Transit of Saturn in the 12th house to natal (birth) Moon: -

Saturn in the 12th house will be defined as a period of less in general. The native will face humiliation or the native's family will face humiliation because of the native. There can be 81 probabilities of planetary conjunctions/combinations when Saturn and Moon are evaluated.

Transit of Saturn over the natal (birth) Moon sign/Rasi: -

This is the transit of a slow-moving yearly planet over a fast-moving monthly planet and that of a dark planet over that of a luminaire.

Saturn's movement over each sign is designated with a name attaching that much importance to its transit, but all planets are extending their part through their association with transiting planet. Hence the mere fear about Sade-Sati need not be pressed upon.

Those who are very hard working and without greed, and with self-confidence will get the support of Saturn during this golden period and they will get new business and new job opportunities.

Those who understand the basic concept the of Sade-Sati transit of Saturn will stand benefited.

During this transit, the position of the Moon should be taken into account from the natal chart to check whether it is in waxing or waning Moon, as this causes considerable changes in Sade-Sati results. Saturn's position in the natal (birth) chart should be ascertained.

The Moon's conjunction/association with malefic, inimical planets should be assessed along with the connection of currently running Maha Dasha (Dasha), Anthat Dasha (Bukthi) in tandem with the Seven-and-a-half-year transit results to conclude the bhavas affected by it. Such an analytical conclusion about the impact of seven-and-a-half-year results will be the complete one and will be in order. Otherwise, it will exhibit only 10% common results. The role of Saturn through its Seven-and-a-half-year transit in improving astrology is important.

Example: -

<table>
<tr><td></td><td></td><td></td><td></td><td></td><td></td><td></td><td></td></tr>
<tr><td></td><td rowspan="2" colspan="2" align="center">Person 1
Misfortune
2 Times</td><td></td><td></td><td rowspan="2" colspan="2" align="center">Person 2
Misfortune
4 Times</td><td></td></tr>
<tr><td></td><td></td><td></td><td></td></tr>
<tr><td></td><td></td><td>Moon 28°
Rahu 26°</td><td></td><td></td><td>Mars 29°</td><td>Moon 21°
Rahu 26°</td><td></td></tr>
</table>

Person 1: -

In the above natal chart, Moon is posited in Libra at 28° and Rahu at 26° and the transit Saturn is moving from Virgo and entering Libra beginning the second leg of the Sade-Sati period. Here, the transit Saturn is not connecting with Moon directly as Rahu is placed in between altering the results. As Saturn has met Rahu first, it will confer lethal sequences, difficulties and losses at first in Libra and will shed a little more while leaving the Libra sign.

Person 2: -

In the above natal chart, Moon is posited in Libra at 21° and Rahu at 28° and the transit Saturn is moving from Virgo and entering Libra beginning the second leg of the Sade-Sati period. Here, the transit Saturn is connecting with Moon which was already impacted by Rahu, altering the results. As Saturn has met Rahu first, it will confer lethal sequences, difficulties and losses at first in Libra and will shed more while leaving Libra sign as all the more malefic planet Mars is posited in Scorpio, in its sign. The impact will be more lethal and ultimate in Sade-Sati.

Example: -

Person 3 chart:

	Person 3 Fortune 10%		
		Jupiter 19° Moon 28°	

Person 4 chart:

	Person 4 Fortune 40%		
		Moon 28° Jupiter 29°	

Person 3: -

For the above native, Moon is in the Visaka asterism (star) of Jupiter and Jupiter is posited in the Swati asterism (star) of Rahu and the transit Saturn is moving from Virgo and entering Libra beginning the second leg of the Sade-Sati period. Here, the transit Saturn is not connecting with Moon directly as Jupiter is placed in between altering the results. **As Saturn has met Jupiter at first, it will confer good fortunes at first in Libra and will not hurt more while leaving the Libra sign due to Sade-Sati.**

Person 4: -

In the above case, both Moon and Jupiter are in the Visaka star in Libra and the transit Saturn is moving from Virgo and entering Libra beginning the second leg of the Sade-Sati period. Here, the transit Saturn is contacting the Moon at first and as there are no planets in between, the native will initially suffer the impact of Sade-Sati and during the exit period of Saturn from Libra the native will enjoy good fortune and will not be impacted by Sade-Sati after that.

The change in results can be felt from the very second of the transit Saturn leaving the Moon and touching Jupiter. This sort of differentiation in declaring the prediction results will enhance the respectability of an astrologer as a result of his experience.

Example: -

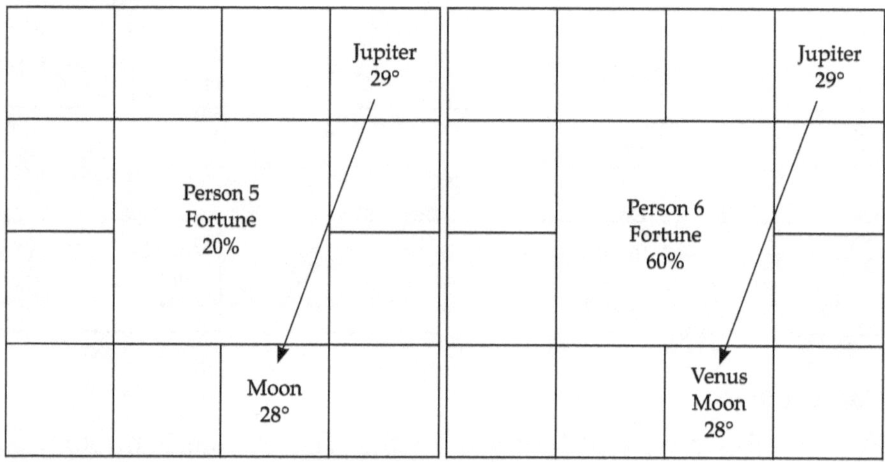

Person 5: -

In his case, the Moon in Libra receives the aspect of Jupiter from Gemini and the transit Saturn is moving from Virgo and entering Libra beginning the second leg of the Sade-Sati period. Here, the transit Saturn is under the aspect of Jupiter altering the results of Sade-Sati and the native will enjoy good fortune and will not be highly impacted by Sade-Sati.

Person 6: -

In this case, the Moon in Libra conjoined with Venus receives the aspect of Jupiter from Gemini and the transit Saturn is moving from Virgo and entering Libra beginning the second leg of the Sade-Sati period. Here, the transit Saturn is under the aspect of Jupiter along with Venus altering the results of Sade-Sati and the native will enjoy very good fortune and will not be impacted by Sade-Sati.

It is essential to analyse various positions of the nine planets concerning their position in conjunction, association, connection, aspect, debilitation, exaltation, and combust positions with other planets to judge the impact of Sade-Sati by comparing various charts before arriving at the results to enhance the reputation of an astrologer.

Transit of Saturn over natal (birth) Mars:

This could be termed as the transit of the Kala Purusha (Time personified) lord of hindrances/disadvantages and fortunes as well over the Kala Purusha (Tie personified) lord of the evil 8th house. This period gives fortune and lethal sequences as well. The transit of a yearly planet over a monthly planet retains the result for a longer period.

1. There are possibilities of accidents and it will be more when Mars is associated with its inimical planets giving grave impacts.
2. Matters relating to land, house, and buildings will be delayed indicating the impact of the karagathuvas of Mars resulting in problems.
3. If natal (birth) Rahu/Ketu/Saturn is closely posited degrees to natal Mars, this transit will bring a lethal impact to many and death to a few.
4. If natal (birth) Rahu/Ketu/Saturn is posited in trines to natal Mars, this transit will bring a lethal impact to many and death to a few.
5. During this transit, many have lost at least one of their limbs and some experience rebirth situations/scenarios. This transit is important in giving surgical treatment.
6. If any one of Mars or Saturn is in retrograde motion in the natal chart, transit Saturn will not accept the results extended to natal Mars. Here planetary power plays a vital role.
7. Transit Saturn will extend beneficial results to Mars when associated with a benefic planet and hence need not be feared as only Saturn's malediction power to Mars associated with malefic hurts. If one attempts at doing the karaka-related business/job of Mars with malefic planets, he will face no/ less hard impacts.

Transit of Saturn over natal (birth) Mercury: -

This is the transit of a yearly planet over a monthly planet. Saturn does not impact heavily during its passage over a lonely-positioned Mercury but changes its course when Mercury is associated with other planets.

As a slow mover, Saturn will impact students in their studies, the karaka of Mercury. Saturn's bitterness will be reflected in the form of misunderstanding between lovers, the karaka relations indicated by Mercury.

Mercury, the indicator of vacant land will push those with money at hand to invest to make a profit.

Those who suffer oblivion will face tough problems and unfavourable Maha Dasha (Dasha), and Antar Dasha (Bukthi) will see them get cheated. During favourable Maha Dasha (Dasha), and Antar Dasha (Bukthi) these people will cheat others.

The transit of Saturn over natal (birth) Mercury denotes cheating others or getting cheated and the level depends on the planetary placements of Saturn and Mercury.

Cheating a person and getting cheated by a person is very common during the transit of Saturn and Mercury and it can be observed through the close placements of Saturn and Mercury in the natal (birth) chart and transit as well.

As both these planets are eunuchs in gender, those who have their transit in the 1st, 3rd, 7th, and 11th houses are advised to add vegetables of Mercury attributives in their food.

Transit of Saturn over natal (birth) Jupiter: -

This transit is like a honey bee intending to collect honey from a flower. This is a golden period for the native to augment his basic life resources and its period of continuation depends upon the Maha Dasha (Dasha), and Antar Dasha (Bukthi) currently in operation along with the base strength of Saturn and Jupiter in the natal (birth) chart.

Those looking for job opportunities will land a good job easily. But their ability to do the job and stick to it will depend on the strength of other planets.

The native will get elevated to a higher level in his life during this transit based on other planets in the natal chart.

If Jupiter and Saturn acquire evil significators based on their bhava positions, this transit will be a period of imprisonment, chronic diseases, and death. As Jupiter is the lord of the 11th house – inflictor of crimes and Saturn is the lord of the evil 8th house for Gemini ascendant, their transit will cause irreparable harm and force them to commit punishable offences.

This planetary association in the natal (birth) chart pushes death during the transit of a similar combination but gives a silent death.

This transit gives not only a higher source of living but also imparts diseases by their acquisition significators.

Ketu's association with this transit gives chronic diseases. Problems like Liver complications, rheumatism, brain damage, and inconsistent heart functions will push the native towards death.

Transit of Saturn over natal (birth) Venus: –

This refers to the flocking of honeybees to the honeycomb. It allows acquiring basic amenities and resources swiftly with the support of a yearly planet over a monthly planet.

The increasing economic support empowers to accumulation of immovable properties as this transit helps in improving economic conditions more than any other period.

If this happens to be the Maha Dasha (Dasha), Antar Dasha (Bukthi) of Venus, it will give fortune of wealth and other life supports.

Wealthy people who are looking for a business will get one. Many people will scale high in their life.

Homemakers should be careful with their servants as they will lure them to marry giving false promises and seductive utterances. It will be a period of compulsion to believe subordinates/servants.

Elderly ladies in the family who are running death-inflicting periods will face death and the position of Venus in low degrees or high degrees will give painful death.

This can also be a golden period which has to be determined based on the strength of these two planets in the natal (birth) chart.

Transit of Saturn over natal (birth) Saturn: -

It is like coming up after a bath from the deep sea. The transit Saturn will increase or decrease the benefits that are due by natal (birth) Saturn by giving struggles and changes in business/job.

Had the natal Saturn been posited in the 2nd house or connected to the 2nd house by aspect or conjunction, the native will face humiliation during the transit of Saturn over the 2nd house or connect with the 2nd house which may be due to love affairs or debt or family situations. Many even migrate from their hometown to other places.

The intensity of the humiliation will be based on the strength of the natal (birth) Saturn which may vary but is sure to happen.

Transit of Saturn over natal (birth) Rahu: -

This transit is something like walking with footwear of thorns. It is the travel of a yearly planet over another yearly planet which is permanently inimical against each other with temporary friendship.

Saturn is traversing over a more powerful planet which uproots big tree-like families and causes separation in joint families.

This is like the native getting caught in a ball of barbed wire and gives the feeling of falling from a high building. If caution is not exercised in practical life, the native will cease to exist.

Many people have gone into hiding and absconded and many billionaires have become paupers during this transit. One in a thousand people without greed succeeded in this transit.

During this transit, a close relative of the native will die. It will be a period of struggle even to get a nominal income and will force to earn through illegal ways.

There is a question as to whether Rahu is inimical or friendlier to Saturn as the answer stands divided.

Which one is right?

During the transit of Rahu over Saturn, situations will warrant the expansion of the business but it ends in irreparable loss which confirms Rahu's inimical nature to Saturn. This is like cutting a piece of cloth with a pair of scissors which does not imply that the cloth is facing expansion unless the cloth is stitched back into a usable material and finally used by someone. For such usage, Jupiter or Venus should aspect Rahu to show a friendlier position. Here too, only the aspect of Jupiter and Venus embarks and hence Rahu stands aloof and not friendlier to Saturn which is my perception. Hence, in my view, Rahu is only inimical to Saturn.

The purported business expansion induced by Rahu is only an illusion and not real.

The native's attention is drawn towards facing hurdles voluntarily during this transit and before he realises the reason is his greed, the hurdles are felt.

The impact will be less when the 'money for work done' policy is adopted without big investments, as it will imply a reduction/loss in profit.

If they expose/reveal their source of income, the income will get subsidised or stopped in full as it will be a period of hurdles/ hindrances in business.

Transit of Saturn over natal (birth) Ketu: -

It is a transit of a planet of wisdom over a half-ascetic planet as both jointly push one towards asceticism. As the Karmic planet is mowed over by the planet for wisdom, it enables the native to energise through wisdom to not lose confidence through karmic impact.

The native will move towards spirituality. Laziness will haunt and the mind will be insensible towards an active life.

The native would have enjoyed his fortunes before the transit and his balanced mind during that period will see him sail through this eventful period without any big impact.

The karaka and bhava significators of Saturn will be affected during this transit.

Those who are engaged in the karaka occupations/businesses relating to Ketu will not be impacted and when do the karaka jobs/businesses of other planets will be severely affected.

Many live with endurance even after a big impact in life for the sake of living and money is very hard to come by as Ketu is the karaka for getting rid of money.

Occupations like tailoring, textile mills, winding, wiring, Doctors, and yarn business are not affected and temple employees and mutts/monasteries as well.

This planetary transit leaves many families divided and parting ways.

Many leave their big businesses due to heavy losses and engage themselves in lower-paid jobs/occupations.

This transit will impound all skills of a person and make him strive for an even smaller income. It drives them to look for money through illegal ways and stops any business improvement.

The difference in transit of Rahu – Saturn: -

Let us see the difference between the transit of Saturn over natal (birth) Rahu and the transit of Rahu over natal (birth) Saturn by comparing two natal charts as an example.

Person 1: -

This person has Rahu posited in Virgo and Saturn has entered Virgo in transit. During this period, he borrowed in excess to expand his well-running business. After expansion, the business faced seizure as he was unable to repay the loan taken. His failure is a Self-invited one.

Person 2: -

This native has Saturn in Sagittarius and Rahu has entered Sagittarius and his business is carrying on well. But during this transit period, there were labour problems, unavailability of raw materials, and competition in the business due to price escalation forcing the native to stop his business. His sufferings are totally due to external factors and not his own. This is the difference between both the transits. In both transits, the natives are affected but remaining without greed lowers the intensity of the impact and related problems.

As both the nodes Rahu and Ketu are shadow planets, the problems extended by them will not be exposed/come to light.

21.

Rahu in Transit

Lord Rahu Gayathri:

Ohm Sirupaya vidhmahe

Amru desaya deemahi

Thanno Rahu prachodayath

Let Lord Rahu bestow his blessings to understand all his Karakathuvas and results.

Transit Results: -

It should be clearly understood that whenever Rahu traverse over other planets and other planets pass over Rahu, the karaka relations, parts, places, and occupation/business relating to Rahu will be affected giving bad results or reduced good results to the native.

22.

KARAKATHUVAS OF RAHU

Rahu in General: -

Rahu is a yearly planet and the transit results exhibited by it will last for a long time. As Rahu is inimical to almost all planets, there will be fewer benefits and more bad results. Those who gained through Rahu are very less and Rahu's transit gives a change of character.

Rahu ruins the character and its transit transforms many good people turns to bad and drives many people to obviate/relocate. The planet associated with Rahu will get a temporal change in its attitude. When there is no planet in the sign of its transit, Rahu will not harm.

When a planet is present in a sign, Rahu's transit over that sign disrupts the planet and the bhava as well. This refers to a change in attitude, religious conversion, foreign travel, jail term, and deportation - the lethal karakas of Rahu.

Rahu in relations: -

Both maternal and paternal Grandfathers (Rahu's presence in male sign, male Navamsa indicates paternal Grandfather and in female sign, female Navamsa indicates maternal Grandfather and both in mixed formations)

Rahu in parts of the body/disease: -

Skin allergy, itching skin, eczema, leukaemia, fits, and surgeries for serious medical complications can be identified by Rahu's placement.

Rahu in places: -

Places where holes, pits, hives, and creepers are present.

Rahu in Deities: -

Deities without a human head, Goddess Durga.

Rahu in materials/products: -

Shining materials.

Rahu in business/occupation: -

Finance, pawn brokering, cinema, photography, medical laboratories, witchcraft/remedial astrology, sorcery, research of aeroplanes, electrical works, watch repair, radio repair, new inventions, representative jobs, T.V repair, cheating, toxic treatment, magic, anti-government activities, smuggling, Glass, porcelain products, exports and imports, overseas manpower,

Blemish by the impact of Rahu: -

Rahu who is lonely placed will not harm in a big way and only when associated with Mars, Venus, and Moon causes blemishes in marriage and others. Rahu is the indicator of blemish and lethal consequences. Through the bhava and its associated planets, Rahu exhibits the blemish.

Rahu's transit: -

Rahu takes 18 days to cross over 1 degree and 2 months to pass over one part of an asterism (star). It takes approximately 18 months to travel through a sign and 18 years to complete one circle of the zodiac.

Transit of Rahu over natal (birth) Sun: -

This is something like covering the light with an umbrella. All the karakathuvas of the Sun will be affected. If the natal chart has the Sun and Rahu combination, Rahu's approach in a similar situation in transit will prove fatal to the father as there will be a botheration to the karaka of the Sun. But there will be changes in the karaka of Rahu which will give beneficial results.

Father if alive, will be affected or his active son will be affected to establish the fact that the native's karaka relations will be affected to give pain to the native.

Administrators/Managers who support the natives will be affected and officials who extended the loans to the native will be targeted.

The father of the native will accumulate unnecessary loans making it difficult to repay or forced to pay exorbitant interest.

Many will be forced to borrow higher rates of interest for administrative reforms but in vain. Change of administration is the option available to keep the respect.

The Sun is considered a respectable planet and he will be tainted when Rahu passes over bringing disrepute.

The native will be attracted towards politics and will force to talk ill of others which should be avoided. The Sun should be accompanied by Saturn during the attraction towards politics.

Example: –

	Sun Rahu 1st Son				Rahu		
	Birth				Transit Rahu		
			Sun Rahu Father				Rahu
Sun Rahu 2nd Son				Rahu			

A person had two sons and for both of them, the Sun and Rahu are conjoined in their natal (birth) charts. The 2nd Son who had the Sun and Rahu combination in Sagittarius is very affectionate towards his father. His father died during the **transit of Rahu in Sagittarius.**

1st Son experienced untold miseries during **the transit of Rahu over his natal Sun and Rahu combination in Aries.**

As the father had the Sun and Rahu combination in Leo, he secured a post in politics during the **transit of the Sun over Rahu** and enjoyed it considerably. He lost his post during **the transit of Rahu over the natal Sun.**

When two incidents occur within a year, the results vary according to Maha Dasha (Dasha), and Antar Dasha (Bukthi), which should be differentiated accordingly for consideration.

Example: -

Ascendant				Ascendant			
	Birth Person 1				Birth Person 2		
		Sun (Uthra-Phalguni)					Sun (Hastham)

Person 1: -

For this Pisces ascendant native, lord of the 6th Sun is in Uthra-Phalguni star in Virgo. During the transit of Rahu over the Sun, he had pain in his back for which a minor surgery was performed and he recovered after 10 months of mental torture and physical suffering. Here the Sun refers to the spine.

Person 2: -

This native of Pisces ascendant, the 5th house lord of Kala Purusha (Time personified) the Sun is in the asterism (star) Hastham of the Moon, lord of the 5th sign Cancer to the ascendant. During the transit of Rahu over the Sun in Rahu Maha Dasha (Dasha), he suffered back pain. He underwent surgery for apprentices. After the surgery, he suffered problems with the food pipe. He struggled for eleven months and recovered after that.

Basic predictions like medical expenses, small obstacles, reduced income, and increased expenditure will be correct when Rahu is passing over the Sun, but it will be 100% precise by computing the placement of the planet, the sign and the star in which it is posited.

Transit of Rahu over natal (birth) Moon: -

This is the worst period of poisoning milk which causes severe problems for all types of people. All sorts of problems will crop up. The native will be afraid of witchcraft, voodoo, sorcery and Blackmagic and will feel the pain. This transit will affect everybody equally. As the Moon indicates mother and mind either of these will be affected. Either the native or his mother will be affected.

1. The native/mother will have mental fear and eye veins will be affected.
2. Poisonous bite through creatures or skin allergy will affect the body turning the skin to dark blue colour.
3. The native/mother will meet with death in case of a period of death or meet lethal sequences.
4. The native/mother will suffer severe problems/loss. In case they have not been affected, then the mother-in-law or elderly women will be affected.
5. For many foods will turn into poison and affect health.
6. Male members will suffer diseases relating to the rectum, abdomen, and skin. Ladies will have uterus problems and roughly 90% of women get surgical treatment for uterus problems.
7. Elderly women will abuse their in-laws and have to avoid confrontation.

Transit Rahu over natal (birth) Mars: -

This is a transit of an undue inimical yearly planet over its enemy planet which produce immediate results. As Mars is the evil 8th house planet of the Kala Purusha (Time Personified), its impact o the native will be severe.

It is the travel of an insect over blood. Had the natal chart contain afflicted Mars by Rahu, the transit will be vulnerable to a reduction of blood platelet counts and calcium and increased joint pain.

This transit may cause dental problems to many who may opt for extraction of teeth.

There will be a change in the character of the karakathuva relations of Mars and those who are already bad will turn worse.

There will be widespread viral fever.

Women will face the worst transit as they will face unbearable problems and pain through their husbands or brothers. Property disputes and vehicular problems will emerge. Their security will be under threat. Ladies who have no property will face problems through their relations as Mars is the indicator of blood relations.

Below given is a birth chart of a family of five members and all of them have the Mars + Rahu combination. During the transit of Rahu in Pisces, the Government notified in Gazette of the acquisition of their land for highway extension. The native's family initiated legal proceedings against the acquisition but could not succeed in the case. Now, during the transit of Rahu in Libra, the court upheld the decision of the Government in the acquisition of the land as valid and advised them to receive the compensation.

<table>
<tr><td>Mars +
Rahu
Person 1</td><td></td><td></td><td></td></tr>
<tr><td>Mars +
Rahu
Person 2</td><td rowspan="2" colspan="2" align="center">Birth</td><td></td></tr>
<tr><td>Mars +
Rahu
Person 3</td><td></td></tr>
<tr><td>Mars +
Rahu
Person 4</td><td>Mars +
Rahu
Person 5</td><td></td><td></td></tr>
</table>

What does this say?

The family's entire joint landed property is lost. For those who are not part of the joint family and did not have the Mars + Rahu combination in their natal (birth) chart are not at the loss of their land.

Person 1: -

For a Sagittarius ascendant female, both Mars and Rahu are in the same asterism (star). She lost her husband in an accident during the Mars Maha Dasha (Dasha) when transit Rahu was passing over natal (birth) Mars.

Person 2: -

For another Sagittarius ascendant female, both Mars and Rahu are in the same asterism (star). When She was running Rahu Maha Dasha (Dasha), during the transit of Rahu over natal Mars, her husband got separated and married another woman.

Person 3: -

For yet another Sagittarius ascendant female, both Mars and Rahu are in the same asterism (star). Rahu was transiting over natal (birth) Mars but no Mars or Rahu Maha Dasha (Dasha) was in operation.

She had no complaints except physical strain as problems surface only if Maha Dasha (Dasha) of Mars or Rahu is in operation during the transit of Rahu. In the absence of the relative transiting planet Maha Dasha (Dasha), and Antar Dasha (Bukthi) in operation, its impact will be very less.

Example: –

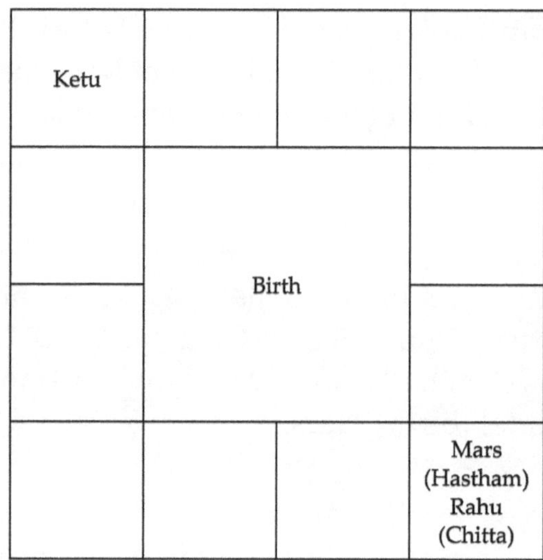

The native of the above natal (birth) chart had Mars and Rahu in the Virgo sign and indicating a deficiency in blood cells. He was running Mars Maha Dasha (Dasha), Moon Antar Dasha (Bukthi), Mercury Prithyantar Dasha (Anthram), and Rahu Sookshma Dasha (Sookshmam). In the natal chart, in Mercury sign, Virgo Mars is placed in the Moon's star conjoined with Rahu in Mars's star constituting the Maha Dasha (Dasha), Antar Dasha (Bukthi), Prithyantar Dasha, and Sookshma Dasha.

Mars is posited in low degrees and Rahu is in high degree than Mars afflicting Mars in its Karakathuva.

Transit of Rahu over natal (birth) Mercury: –

Rahu is transiting over Mercury which is considered eviler than Rahu in giving results. As Mercury is the karaka for skin, this transit may cause skin-related diseases.

Mercury represents veins and Rahu indicates itching. Viral infections will affect blood veins and may cause itching in the skin.

Black spots will appear on the face due to variations in blood circulation. The native will have serious thoughts and become smart.

Mercury is the lord of love and Rahu is problematic. Hence those who are into lovemaking should be careful to avoid unnecessary problems to avoid any love break. New acquaintances will push towards bad habits.

Mercury denotes education and Rahu denotes obstruction. Hence this transit will cause obstruction in studies and devoid of higher education.

The maternal uncle is the karaka of Mercury and Rahu's dangerous situations. If the native is very affectionate towards any of his maternal uncles', he will be facing death-like situations and may have to leave him. Good friendships will face stigma.

Mercury represents vacant land and Rahu causes encumbrance. The transit flares up the already existing encumbrances in the vacant land and interference of third parties in those land.

Transit of Rahu over natal (birth) Rahu: -

It is the travel of a poisonous creature over a living thing. As this is a transit of a yearly planet over a yearly planet, the decisions taken during the transit will carry its impact for a longer duration. There will be some mistakes in any of the actions taken or mistakes can be found in the performance.

The native will be branded as a scoundrel by somebody.

It is an ideal time for IVF – In Vitro Fertilisation – to have children through artificial ways, as Rahu indicates artificial means. During this transit children will face health issues. Blemishes in the natal (birth) chart due to the impact of ancestor's wows, deeds will increase or may crop up.

The native will be forced to seek the bad company of people voluntarily and if caution is not exercised it will result in a huge loss. A close relative's death may occur.

This transit will force them to go for quick money and will get cheated and face betrayal. An amount of Rupees 80 lacs invested during the transit of Rahu over natal (birth) Jupiter in good faith was cheated altogether.

Those who borrowed from this person cheated him without repaying and to keep his reputation, this gentleman has to lose his entire property to repay his creditors.

This transit induces an inclination towards financing. As Jupiter denotes muscles, there will be muscle contractions or problems in the skin. There will be small gains but end up in big losses. The native or his children will face lethal occasions or accidents and if the worst Maha Dasha, Antar Dasha (Bukthi) is in operation, may face death.

Child (1) through In Vitro Fertilisation: -

<table>
<tr><td></td><td></td><td></td><td></td><td></td><td></td><td></td><td>Ketu</td></tr>
<tr><td>Moon</td><td rowspan="2">Birth
Husband</td><td>Ketu</td><td></td><td rowspan="2">Birth
Wife</td><td></td></tr>
<tr><td>Rahu</td><td></td><td>Jupiter</td><td></td></tr>
<tr><td>Jupiter</td><td></td><td></td><td>Rahu</td><td>Moon</td><td></td></tr>
</table>

<table>
<tr><td></td><td></td><td>Ketu</td></tr>
<tr><td></td><td rowspan="2">Transit</td><td></td></tr>
<tr><td>Jupiter</td><td></td></tr>
<tr><td>Rahu</td><td>Moon</td><td></td></tr>
</table>

Rule: Both Jupiter and Rahu are the Karaka lords for test tube babies and only their link in the natal (birth) chart can give success in begetting a healthy child through artificial insemination medical treatment. In the above natal (birth) charts, Jupiter is in Sagittarius and Rahu in Capricorn for the Husband and Jupiter in Capricorn and Rahu in Sagittarius for the wife.

The couple underwent treatment to beget a child artificially during the transit of Rahu in Capricorn and Jupiter in Sagittarius and they had a beautiful child during the transit of Jupiter in Capricorn and Rahu in Sagittarius. Positioning of Rahu ahead of Jupiter during childbirth indicates a blemish in progeny showing deficiency in vigour.

Child (2) through In Vitro Fertilisation: -

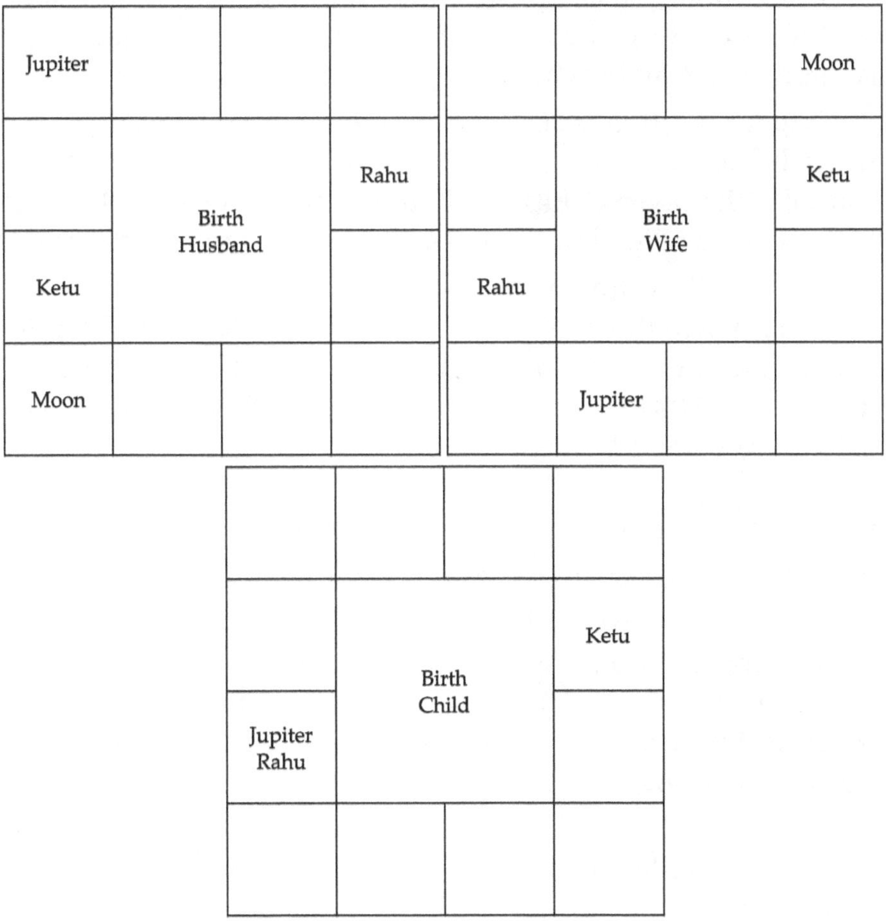

Birth Husband

Jupiter			
	Rahu		
Ketu			
Moon			

Birth Wife

			Moon
			Ketu
Rahu			
	Jupiter		

Birth Child

			Ketu
	Jupiter Rahu		

Rule: Both Jupiter and Rahu are the Karaka lords for test tube babies and only their link in the natal (birth) chart can give success in begetting a healthy child through artificial insemination medical treatment.

In the husband's natal chart, Jupiter is in Pisces and Ketu in Capricorn and Rahu in Cancer receiving the aspect of Jupiter. In the natal chart of the wife, Rahu is in Capricorn and Ketu is in Cancer receiving the aspect of Jupiter in Scorpio.

The couple had a beautiful child during the transit of Jupiter and Rahu in Capricorn and Ketu in Cancer receiving the aspect of Jupiter.

Jupiter in the natal chart of both the husband-and-wife aspect and the other mutually ensures a good result.

In the family chart of all three, Jupiter is not in a hidden position of 6th, 8th, or 12th and Rahu and Ketu are in the same sign as Capricorn in all the charts.

To get a positive result, Rahu should transit over natal Jupiter in the husband's natal (birth) chart or the wife's natal (birth) chart. On the reverse, Jupiter should transit over natal Rahu in the husband's natal (birth) chart of the Wife's natal (birth) chart.

The medical treatment for In Vitro Fertilisation proves successful when the transit Saturn aspect the natal (birth) Jupiter or transit Jupiter aspect natal (birth) Saturn in either of husband or wife's natal (birth) chart. In my experience, 80% success is seen during this planetary combination.

Transit of Rahu over natal (birth) Venus: –

This refers to the transit of a yearly planet over a benefic monthly planet giving instant results to the native.

This transit will bring in sudden fortunes as desires will be exposed in the vision. Uncontrolled desires will result in heavy losses as the fortunes will bring in less but take away even legitimate earnings in a big way.

Women at home will have wrong thoughts and will be involved in an illegitimate friendship or bad company resulting in evil actions and bad results. It will force them to join unwanted and support unnecessary companies. Women at home will face health issues.

The presence of Venus + Rahu combination, association or aspect in the natal (birth) chart will cause problems to gents by ladies and through relatives to women.

Had Venus and Rahu been associated in the natal (birth) chart with Venus in an afflicted position, the native will suffer at a young stage and in middle age if unafflicted.

Many will migrate or obviate from their native place or suffer imprisonment due to unbearable suffering because of excessive greed and denote expenditures on unknown things.

Improbable and unknown things like extracting power from the debris of thunder, barium, treasure hunt, and treatment to maintain youth forever, will drive the natives to spend huge money unnecessarily.

Caution should be exercised during the Maha Dasha (Dasha), Antar Dasha (Bukthi) of Venus, Saturn, and Rahu/Ketu to avoid such vicious actions.

Transit of Rahu over natal (birth) Saturn: -

It is the transit of a speed-breaking yearly planet's transit over the conductor of life, another yearly planet Saturn. This transit drives the native slowly through unending greed to a point making survival a big question mark. As this transit involves two yearly planets, their results and aftermath will continue even after the transit comes to an end. Those who are expecting big results should remain calm and composed as this transit will extend unending enmity, unending problems, and unpayable loans.

This transit resembles something like making a person vomit his entire intake after feeding his belly full. There will be the death of a close relative.

The native will face situations to expand his business but once ventured into expansion, the business may face a stoppage due to the inability of supervision and maintenance. The business may face crucial problems forcing a change in the business/profession.

Had there been any conjunction or connection between Saturn and Rahu in the natal (birth) chart, the impact will continue during this transit.

Ancestral properties will cause misunderstandings between the relations. The benefits or income hitherto received from the family properties by the native or extended by the native to the family will be denied.

This transit will bring a bad name to the native and unless caution is exercised it will force the native to obviate/migrate to other towns/places.

Those who have Saturn + Rahu combination in 1st, 3rd, 7th, and 11th bhavagas hoping do a revolutionary marriage will end up marrying uncharacteristically.

Many big traditional families failed miserably and were doomed during this transit period as this transit pushes one towards an unimagined life.

Those who want to amaze wealth in unscrupulous ways unmindful of the punishment will get their desires fulfilled.

The native may be trapped in accidents, lethal sequences and even death if unfavourable Maha Dasha (Dasha), and Antar Dasha (Bukthi) are in operation if they have Saturn and Rahu combination in natal (birth) chart in the same closeness as in transit. Here closeness can be presumed as from 1° extending to the successive signs.

This transit may cause fractures in the hands/legs compelling bandages in the hands/legs for quite some time during this transit.

As the proverb 'Problems in succession' indicates, there will be constant suffering in the bhava-related events in which this transit takes place.

If there is a planet associated with natal (birth) Saturn in the natal (birth) chart, during transit Rahu will conjoin Saturn and become friends to close off the associated planet first and then will fight among themselves to give their ill effects.

Transit of Rahu over natal (birth) Rahu: -

It is like recouping after exhausting the energy after a marathon. Rahu after spitting the poison it had in the pouch has now come to refill it.

This transit will topple life. If there is a planet in the adjacent sign of Rahu in the natal (birth) chart, then during transit Rahu affects that planet's karaka and its significators.

Let us look at some examples to establish the same: -

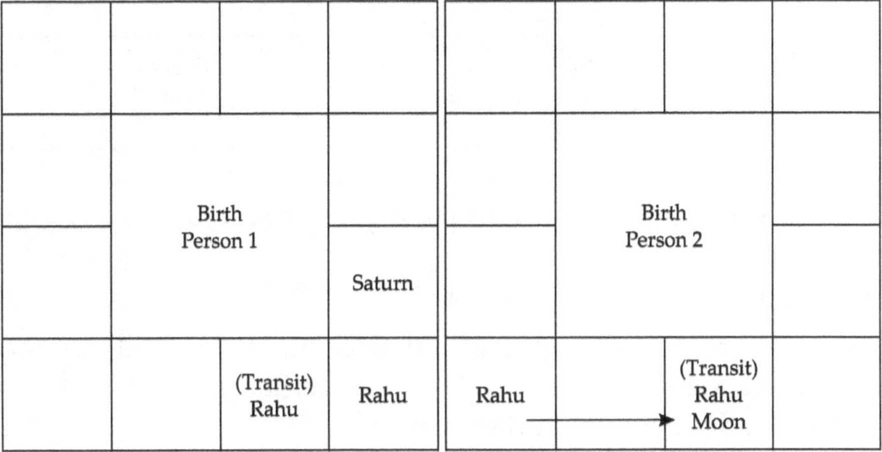

Person 1: -

Saturn is in Leo and Rahu in Virgo is moving towards Leo. Transiting Rahu in Libra starts bothering Saturn in Leo through its natal position in Virgo and once it joins natal (birth) Rahu, it mounts more pressure and problems on Saturn in Leo.

Person 2: -

Rahu in its transit of Libra bothers the natal Moon in Libra much more as natal (birth) Rahu touches the natal Moon first in its motion even though it is posited two signs away from it. Instigating its effect in its transit.

Example: -

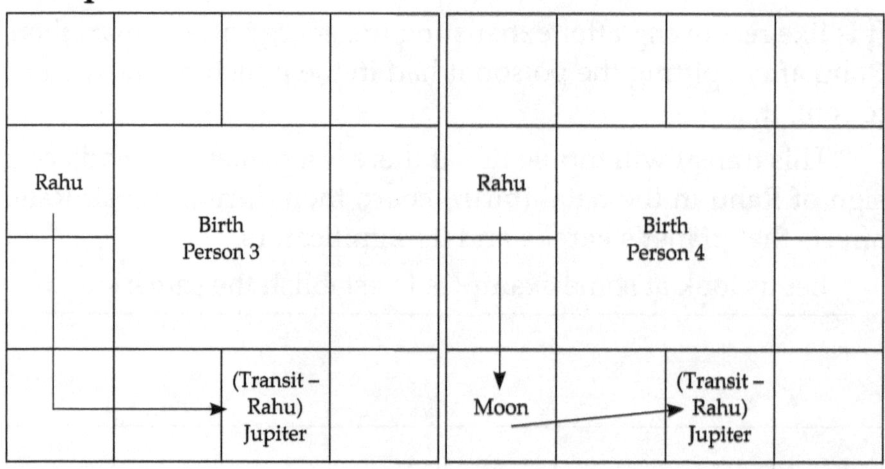

Both persons 3 and 4 have Rahu in Aquarius and Jupiter in Libra.

Person 3: -

As there are no other planets in between Rahu and Jupiter, the transit Rahu impacts Jupiter severely fiercely and with his characteristics devoid of other planets.

Person 4: -

In this case, the Moon is placed in between the natal (birth) Jupiter in Libra and Rahu in Aquarius, thereby filtering the impact but including the characteristic of the Moon in it.

It is very important to understand the distance between the planets to judge the results as to which planet the transiting planet has passed over and the planet it is about to impact.

23.

THE KARAKA DIFFERENCES BETWEEN RAHU AND KETU

Rahu	Ketu
Loss	Difficulty
Party	Campaign/Community
Corruption	Anti-Corruption
Scissors	Needle/Injection
Illegal	Legal
Chop	Punch
Crime	Punishment
Yoga	Penance
Dance/Make merry	Calm
Fake	Real
Win	Fire
Salvation	Wisdom
Causing Problems	Causing Separation
Beginning	End
End	Beginning

Rahu	Ketu
Lethal sequences (Big)	Lethal sequence (small)
Red patches (hives) disease	Black patches (hives) disease
Will Chop one	Will bundle out
Big	Small
Small Court/Village Panchayat	Big Court
Will Unite	Will Separate
Multiple Squares	Multiple Stripes
Speech	Silence. Breath
Beard	Moustache
Canine tooth	Dental occlusion/Tooth decay
More than one	Less than one
Exposed theft	Hidden Theft
Steal	Take/Pick-up
Religion	Spiritual path
Gun in the hands of the terrorists	Gun in the hands of the Police/Military
Medical treatment	Medical tests
Prosecution/Subject to tests	Judgement/Punishment
Demonstration	Peace
Riot/Commotion	Hunger Strike
Political procession	Funeral procession

24.

KETU IN TRANSIT

Lord Ketu Gayathri:

Ohm Amwathwajaya vidhmahe

Soolahasthaya deemahi

Thanno Ketu prachodath

Let Lord Ketu bestow his blessings to understand all his Karakathuvas and results.

Transit Results: –

It should be clearly understood that whenever Ketu traverse over other planets and other planets pass over Ketu, the karaka relations, parts, places, and occupation/business relating to Ketu will be affected giving bad results or reduced good results to the native.

25

KARAKATHUVAS OF KETU

Ketu in General: -

All legal and complicated things. Ketu causes separation among relations.

Ketu in relations/persons: -

Both paternal and maternal Grandmothers {Masculine Sign, Masculine Navamsa (Paternal side) Grandmothers} [Feminine Sign, Feminine Navamsa (Maternal side) Grandmothers] and both in alternatives.

Ketu in parts of the body/diseases: -

The complicated nervous system, unidentified diseases.

Ketu in places: -

Courtrooms, Legal Chambers, Lawyers assembly room/hall/bar council, tailoring shop, weaving centres, Knitting centres.

Ketu as Deities: -

Lord Ganesh, Deity without a human face but with a tail.

For example, Shri Hanuman, and Shri Sarabeswarar.

Ketu in things: -

Very thin strings, electrical wires/cables, threads, needles/injections.

Ketu in marital relations: -

There is not much difference between Rahu and Ketu except that Rahu will propel mistakes that cannot be justified whereas those instigated by Ketu can be justified. Rahu will cause gaucheries/ uglier scenes in marital relations and Ketu relates to problems arising in marital relations leading to compromise/actions/ interventions through Panchayat, Police stations and Court.

Ketu in Profession/Business/Job: -

Weaving, tailoring, Lawyer/Advocate, Compromise/Counseling, winding, wiring, typist, Surgeons, tobacco, cotton, tea, coffee beans, pharmacy, medical labs, spiritual, devotional products selling shops, orthodoxy rituals performers, death sentence executioners along with those mentioned for Rahu. Sorcery/ witchcraft, cement, rubber industries, and domicile in foreign countries are also indicated by Ketu.

Transit Ketu: -

Ketu takes 18 days to pass over 1° and 2 months to cross one part of an asterism (star). It takes a year and a half to sail through a sign and takes 18 years to complete the zodiac.

Ketu does not have any aspect but controls the 3rd and 11th signs from where it stands. It impacts its full power to the planet it is about to touch when it is as close as 21° from that planet. The native who has the blessings of God is not impacted by the passing over of Ketu.

Being a yearly planet, the transit results of Ketu will last long and as there are more inimical planets, benefic results from Ketu will be less and malefic results will be more. People who have gained through Ketu are very minimal.

Ketu extends good or bad results in its Maha Dasha (Dasha) and Antar Dasha (Bukthi) period only and does not do any good during its transit.

Had there been any planet associated with Ketu, their combined Maha Dasha (Dasha), Antar Dasha (Bukthi), and Prithyantar Dasha (Anthram) will give good or bad results depending on the bhava in which they are posited and the planet's benefic/malefic character.

If a planet is positioned in the sign in which Ketu transits, there will be some benefits and a planet in the trines to the sign in which Ketu transits will indicate the crisis the native is about to face.

If there are any planets in the 1st, 10th, and 19th stars in which Ketu transits, they will face the impact. As Ketu do not have a house of its own, it assumes possession of the house in which it transits.

Ketu forbids the karakathuva results of the planet over which it transits.

If the planet over which the Ketu transits performs the karaka-related actions/jobs of Ketu, then Ketu will support highly such actions/jobs with favourable results.

The moment Ketu crosses the planet, the problems faced by the native will get reduced/stopped and the impact created by Ketu may end abruptly or carry over for a few years.

It can be related to the time of healing of the wound caused by Ketu less or more depending on the size.

Ketu is a node of fire and he must cleanse anything close to him. As he is also a node of wisdom, he imparts wisdom to any planet over which he passes over or the planet that passes over him.

Ketu is responsible for many to become saints, sages, and yogis. It cleanses the deeds and actions of the native and purifies and bestows wisdom.

As Ketu supports asceticism, those who wish to become saints can make use of this transit.

Ketu is a node of revenge and any wrongdoings by the natives will receive punishment. And as Ketu is subject to separation, the natives who fight for separation will get it.

As Ketu do not support money and influence, the natives who are greedy to have money and influence will face struggles.

Greedy natives will face never-ending enmity, irrecoverable loans, and unending problems.

Ketu rules and supports all legal activities and hence any actions carried out legally will succeed.

He looks for laudation.

Ketu equals Saturn in honesty.

Saturn – The Scale, Ketu – the index/scale indicator, Rahu – Chains of the Scale, Other Planets – weighing measures.

If Rahu/Ketu are in the masculine sign in the natal (birth) chart, it takes control of the planets that are entering into the masculine sign.

If Rahu/Ketu are in the feminine sign in the natal (birth) chart, it takes control of the planets that are entering into the feminine sign.

As both the nodes Rahu/Ketu are moving in the opposite direction, the degrees of their motion will reduce gradually and a degree-wise assessment will give pinpointed results.

As Ketu acts as leader of Political parties, Campaigns/community gatherings/movements, it will push interest in those political parties, and Campaigns indicated by the karakathuva of the planet over which Ketu is associated/conjoined and this intensifies in Ketu's transit.

Because of this...

One may have to face imprisonment/confined to jail/face legal implications when Ketu is connected to the 8th bhava.

Ketu's association with the 11th bhava may see elevation to political party posts with intense participation which may result in staying separated from the family.

Transit Ketu will cause unidentified/complicated diseases to those planets afflicted by Ketu in the natal (birth) chart.

Ketu does not harm those without greed but supports and elevates them to unexpected heights in their field of activity.

Ketu and net/trap/knitting:

Ketu denotes net/trap. When transit Ketu passes over the natal (birth) Sun, it throws authoritative commands over the native who stands benefited by remaining without opposing it and harmed when opposes the authority.

During the transit of Ketu over the natal (birth) Moon, stitches may be carried out for wounds/patches or screens may be placed over the eyes (after an eye operation/cataract).

The native will be caught in the web of affection during the transit of Ketu over natal (birth) Mars and in the absence of properties, he will see a new dimension of life through the affectionate.

Transit of Ketu over natal (birth) Mercury weaves a web of love upon the native and it separates those who are already in lover affairs by intensifying the problems amongst the lovers.

The native will be caught in the web of lust/libido, infatuation/ sexual delight, and attractive web of luxurious living during the transit of Ketu over natal (birth) Venus without knowing the depth/intensity of the problems he is involved in.

The native will be attracted towards the spiritual web during the transit of Ketu over natal (birth) Jupiter thus getting relieved from worldly pleasures.

Ketu spins a web of asceticism over the native during its transit over natal (birth) Saturn, but unlike other webs, the native is not easily caught in the web of asceticism.

Transit of Ketu over the natal (birth) Sun: -

This refers to the transit of the planet of wisdom over that of the soul. Liberation of the soul from worldly sins, spiritual incarnation, and enlightenment through spiritual means will be highly favoured throughout this year. As this is the travel of a yearly planet over a monthly planet, severe and sincere training in yoga and the spiritual path will yield good results.

As Ketu refers to campaigns/movements and the Sun to administration/governance, this period will support those indulging in campaigns/movements who will get a good name and fame with increased involvement in the activities but will not give any monetary benefits.

The head of the family will be engaged in spiritual activities. The father of the native will be suffering from eye and neurological disorders indicating complicated deceases. The Sun denotes the head and Ketu refers to complication. This transit indicates complicated deceases in the head of the native or his father or his first son.

Transit Ketu affects the planets posited in the same degrees as natal (birth) Ketu and also those planets which are placed in close degrees by bringing them under its control.

Ketu like intuiting knowledge gives all sorts of problems to the native or his father or his first son.

If The Maha Dasha (Dasha), Antar Dasha (Bukthi) of the Sun or Ketu is in operation during the currency of the Ketu's transit over the Sun (in transit), the impact caused by Ketu will be unbearable and if the star in which Ketu transits or in the 1st, 10th, 19th star in which Ketu transits happens to be where the natal Sun is posited, the aftermath of the impact by Ketu's transit over the natal (birth) Sun will be known now.

Ketu's transit over the transit Sun will indicate what will happen during the transit of Ketu over the natal (birth) Sun beforehand. Exercising caution and a good attitude will save the ensuing problems of Ketu's transit over the natal (birth) Sun.

Transit of Ketu over natal (birth) Moon: -

This transit is like a poisonous creature creeping over a pot of milk. While Rahu spits poison Ketu does not spit poison but just swims over. The native will be caught by the fear of voodoo, witchcraft, sorcery, and wizardry. Everybody is afraid during this transit. As the Moon represents the mind and mother as well, either the native or his mother will be affected.

The native will have mental stress during this transit and those who already have mental stress will face depression leading to health issues and may at times be subject to poisonous bites by creatures/insects/reptiles.

As Ketu remarks law and the Moon to mind and efforts, the transit forces the native/his mother/or both the native and his mother to face trial before justice/judicial consequences.

In the case of female horoscopes, this transit gives a crisis to her husband or indicates that her husband is facing some crisis. In the case of troublesome husbands, it denotes litigation against their husbands, complaints at the police station, and mediation before village heads.

In the case of females, their husbands are affected and even face death if death inflicts Maha Dasha (Dasha), and Antar Dasha (Bukthi) in operation during the currency of the transit. The females suffer from uterus problems, rectum/anus, and or urinary infections.

The devotion towards deities without a human face like, Lord Anjaneya (Maruthi), Lord Ganesha, Goddess Vaarahi, Goddess Prithyankara Devi, and Lord Lakshmi Narasimhar increases.

The native/his mother is attracted towards the spiritual path of wisdom, and devotion towards God thus giving him a good life.

This transit forces the native to believe the legal remedy is the only option for all his problems unwilling to compromise on litigations.

As the Moon indicates, the body and food digestive system and Ketu to karaka for web/knit, some of the natives have to protect their abdomen/stomach by having a filter in the intestine to protect it.

As the Moon represents the body and Ketu sharp-edged articles/weapons, some of the natives are attacked by these sharp-edged weapons/articles or pierced by these particles in an accident. Depending upon the placement of the Moon in the sign or bhava, Ketu imparts surgery in those body parts.

Both the nodes Rahu and Ketu differ in minor heads. While Rahu is responsible for blemishes, Ketu gives the punishment or freedom from those blemishes.

202 | Accurate Transit Predictions

When there are no planets in between the natal (birth) Moon and the natal (birth) Ketu, transit Ketu afflicts the Moon severely. If Ketu passes over any other planets before coming into contact with the Moon, then it impacts the Moon with the character of the planet it impacted earlier. This is true based on my experience.

Example: –

	4th house Moon Ketu	Mars			Mars Ketu		
Ascen-dant	Birth				Transit 01-05-2013		
		Rahu				Rahu	

For the above native of Capricorn ascendant, Moon and Ketu are in Aries, the 4th house. He is a natural seeker of justice as he is currently running Mars Maha Dasha (Dasha).

When Ketu approached Aries in transit, he sought legal remedy for a property dispute as Ketu has already crossed over Mars indicating litigations in property matters. He is a Capricorn ascendant born; the property is adjacent to a burial ground.

On the day of consultation, both the Sun and Mars were in Aries and the native prefers an appeal to the Supreme court as the sign Leo indicates lower courts like the District Court and Aries indicates courts in Capital Cities like the High Court and Supreme Court.

As the lord of the 4th house Aries i.e. Mars who is also the lord of the evil to Movable sign Capricorn, these natives will have encumbrance in their properties along with wealth/properties.

As Mars and Ketu are close in the natal (birth) chart, there will be waste/loss of money whenever Ketu crosses/comes closer to Mars in transit and as the native is currently running Mars Maha Dasha (Dasha), he has advised the prevalence of the litigation throughout Mars Maha Dasha (Dasha).

Example: -

Birth chart:

Ascendant		Moon Ketu	4
Jupiter 12	Birth		
	Rahu (6th house to 4th)		

Transit chart:

		Jupiter Ketu	
	Transit		
	Rahu		

In the above natal (birth) chart, the native has both the Moon and Ketu in star Rohini in Taurus. When the native was 17 years old, his mother was having a mental disorder and was treated in a hospital during the transit of Ketu in Taurus.

Again, Ketu transited to Rohini Star in Taurus at his 35th year of age (09-06-2012) causing problems in the lungs of the native requiring hospitalisation in the ICU and recovering after treatment. Though Ketu was posited with Jupiter in transit, it continued its impact.

In the first cycle, During the transit of Ketu over the natal Moon and Ketu, the native was running Rahu Maha Dasha (Dasha) evil lord 6th from 4th house (an indicator of mother). During the 2nd cycle, the native was running Jupiter Maha Dasha (Dasha) during the transit of Ketu over the natal Moon and Ketu. Here Jupiter in the 12th to the ascendant in the natal (birth) chart indicated hospitalisation for treatment and in both cases, the native was in the hospital for self and mother, the karakathuvas of the Moon with the differentiation of the running Maha Dasha.

Example: –

		Moon Wife's sign				Ketu	
	Birth				Transit		
Moon Husband's sign				Rahu			

In the above-combined chart of both the husband and wife, the Moon is in Rohini star in Taurus for the wife and Saturn's star Anuradha (Anusham) in Scorpio.

During the transit of Ketu in Taurus, both the husband and wife had problems between them and opted for separation.

Note: –

When there is the placement of planets on the 1 – 7 axis in a joint family such implications during the transit of Ketu are bound to happen and when more than one such birth chart is afflicted during the transit of Ketu, the entire family faces unbearable suffering.

During the computation of natal (birth) charts to declare results about marriage/divorce, an analysis of the natal charts of both the concerned parties should be done. In case of divorce by two parties, both charts need not show separation, as one of the parties may not be willing to separate, while the other does. This I have discussed at length in my book titled 'Effects of Joint Horoscopes'.

Transit of Ketu over natal (birth) Mars: -

This is the transit of two inimical planets which gives different results in males and females.

In Children: -

Blood-related diseases, smallpox/chicken pox, and boils bother the natives. Many will meet with accidents and suffer injuries and scars.

In Males: -

1. There will be impacts/difficulties in the karakathuvas of Mars like houses, land, vehicles, and male siblings.
2. There may be problems in household duties for servants/ servant maids, drivers through vehicles and mechanics in workshops.
3. There will be misunderstandings between brothers in money matters.
4. Encumbered properties will cause more worries and problems during this transit forcing legal issues, litigation, and complaints in the police stations and court proceedings.
5. Those who are married for years will face impotency during this transit and are likely to go for treatment.

The aspect of Jupiter during this period will see an effective cure in the treatment for impotency and will go against it in the absence of Jupiter's aspect.

In Females: -

1. Their husbands will face problems.
2. If a female is affectionate towards her brother, he will be affected.
3. After long years of marriage, the husbands will become impotent and will undergo treatment. When not affected, they will lose interest in their wives.

These implications will become all right after the transit without any medicine/medical treatment.

General: –

1. The native will have teeth problems. There may be blood-related diseases and bone-marrow-related problems.
2. The problems relating to the karakathuva of Mars will emerge and it will spice up with bhava related in case of adverse Maha Dasha (Dasha), and Antar Dasha (Bukthi). Transit of inimical planets is sure to cause karakathuva-related problems/difficulties whether the Maha Dasha (Dasha) and Antar Dasha (Bukthi) support or not,
3. Those who have a strong Mars in their natal (birth) chart are unable to resist the implications of the transit while those with a weak Mars will sail through.

The position of Mars whether posited alone or conjoined with other planets should be reckoned before declaring the results.

Ideas of Real estate ventures to make a big income and transit of Ketu over natal (birth) Mars…

Example: –

Birth			
Mars			
	Birth		
	Moon		

Transit			
	Ketu 2	Ketu 1	
	Transit		
	Rahu 1	Rahu 2	

For this native, Mars is ruling in Aries and Moon is in the 7th Libra inducing undaunted love towards landed properties.

He bought land during the transit of Ketu in Taurus intending to sell the land before Ketu touches Mars in Aries to make a big money. But he could not sell the land as planned and now he is in a big financial crisis forcing him to sell the land at a throwaway price.

Ketu induced the karakathuva of Mars in Aries in him during Ketu's transit in Taurus. It will be wise to invest with owned funds as Ketu inflicts malefic results when invested with borrowed funds.

The native has to struggle hard to succeed in his attempts reason being the transit of Rahu over the natal Moon in Libra during the transit of Ketu in Aries.

No expansion activities should be attempted relating to the karakathuvas of the planet over which Rahu/Ketu is about to pass over as it will result only in loss/failure.

Example: -

		Venus	Mars Punar-vasu
	Birth Female 1		

		Jupiter	Mars Punar-vasu
	Birth Female 2		

In female natal charts, Mars represents 'Kalathra Karaka' (pointer of spouse/husband). Hence marriage proposals during the transit of Rahu/Ketu over natal (birth) Mars will result in problems.

Overriding this, if marriages are conducted, it will either bring the crisis to the husband or the husband will be in a big crisis.

In both the female charts, Mars is in Punarvasu star belonging to Jupiter and transit Ketu is passing over Gemini.

Female 1: –

In the case of female 1, the transit gave financial difficulties to the husband. As Venus is posited in the 12th house to Mars in Gemini, transit Ketu carried the significators of Venus while passing over Mars.

Female 2: –

In this case, it gave diseases in the body as Jupiter in the 12th house to Mars has become a reason as the star in which Mars is positioned is that of Jupiter. As transit Ketu is crossing over Mars before touching Jupiter, it imparted the significators/karakas of Jupiter along with Mars.

The transit of Ketu over a planet reveals the type of impact it is going to cause through the 12th house planet to Mars.

Example: –

			Mars Ketu				Rahu
	Person 1				Person 2		
Rahu			Mars Ketu				

In marriage matching, there are a Humpty number of invisible ticklish issues in which one is like this planetary combination/compatibility.

The task undertaken jointly by any two has to be scrutinised before execution based on the planetary combination/ compatibility.

Both the above natives joined and put up a project together to build and sell houses for which they collected money from so many.

They could not execute even one portion of their plan though money has been collected. The problem both faced drove them to elope out of the city.

Reason to elope: –

The planetary combination of Mars + Ketu is in Cancer for one and in Capricorn for the other.

They commenced their project while transit Ketu was passing over Leo. When transit Ketu approached the Mars + Ketu combination in the Cancer of one person, it flagged the transit of Rahu over the Mars + Ketu over the other triggering the failure of the karakathuva project of Mars.

It should be noted that a plan/project involving the karakathuva of a planet will face a certain failure someday when that karaka planet is associated/conjoined with the malefic nodes Rahu/Ketu. Only those projects based on the karakathuvas of Rahu/Ketu will augur well with the support of Rahu/Ketu when there is no greed to amaze wealth by illegal means.

Both the natives have an association with Mars, the karakathuva for a house with Ketu the prime reason behind the failure. They planned this project during the presence of Ketu in Leo and have not listened to my advice brushing out saying that the project is by payment in instalments, a karakathuva of Rahu. They intend to earn big fifty times of money through this project and their greed is the cause of their failure.

The one who had exalted Mars in Cancer ran away unable to face the problems. The other with debilitated Mars tried to solve the problems. Debilitated Mars loses its energy while conjunct with inimical planets rather than in a debilitated status.

Mars debilitates at 28° in Cancer and exalts at 28° in Capricorn. But when Mars loses its power once it crosses 28°. Though Capricorn defines Capricorn as South direction as per the Kala Purusha (Time personified), it cannot be construed as fully exalted when Capricorn is not the ascendant from experience. Astrology is a treatise with thousands of knots which can be understood only with the blessings of the Almighty, the supreme God.

Example: –

Birth chart:

Ascendant		Ketu	Mars
	Birth		
Rahu			

Transit chart:

			Ketu
	Transit		
	Rahu		

For this native, Mars is placed in the fourth house Gemini in Rahu's asterism (star) to the Pisces ascendant. Ketu is moving into Gemini from Cancer where Mars debilitates. The native is infected in the blood causing health hazards.

He borrowed money from the bank by pledging his house documents but could not repay the loan. The Bank proceeded legally against him to recover the loan proceeds. So far, the native has not faced any legal issues but this transit has forced him to stand to face legal actions. As Mars is posited in Rahu's star in Mercury's Gemini sign, the native was forced to borrow by pledging his house documents.

Why legal actions?

This is purely due to the transit of Ketu over natal (birth) Mars. The karaka relating to the question Mars has Ketu posited in the 12th house in the natal (birth) chart which is like a viper bite.

As Rahu is in the 6th house to Mars whose star Mars is posited, the native has to suffer by borrowing and legal actions.

Example: -

<table>
<tr><td></td><td></td><td>Mars
Jupiter</td><td></td></tr>
<tr><td rowspan="2"></td><td colspan="2" rowspan="2">Birth</td><td rowspan="2"></td></tr>
<tr></tr>
<tr><td></td><td></td><td></td><td></td></tr>
</table>

<table>
<tr><td></td><td></td><td>Ketu</td><td></td></tr>
<tr><td rowspan="2"></td><td colspan="2" rowspan="2">Transit</td><td rowspan="2"></td></tr>
<tr></tr>
<tr><td></td><td>Rahu</td><td></td><td></td></tr>
</table>

In the above natal (birth) chart, both Mars and Jupiter are in Taurus, and transit Ketu is moving over them.

The native suffered blood pressure and at the same time, he was invited to participate in a noble cause of the construction of a common temple in the village. Though he refused, his selfless service to society forced the general public to compel him to accept the service. His health two deteriorated at the same time.

As both Jupiter and Mars are lords of the trines between them and lords of 2/12 amongst them, their association gave both good and bad together. During the transit of Ketu over this planetary combination both good and bad may surface.

Transit of Ketu over natal (birth) Mercury: -

In Children: -

As there exists enmity between the karaka for tongue Mercury and karaka for nerves Ketu, the small veins in the tongue will be affected in children impairing their speech. There may be bleeding due to cuts/wounds in the nose and tongue. Cheeks may be affected by skin-related diseases.

Mercury denotes education and Ketu refers to blocks/stoppage. The Children's education will see a stoppage/break and children who were securing high marks will score fewer marks during this transit. Those who are already scoring low marks will fail the examinations.

Had this transit been seen during the examination period in sensitive children, they should be closely monitored failing which the children will take wrong decisions due to their indecisive nature and troubled mind. Unfavourable Maha Dasha (Dasha), and Antar Dasha (Bukthi) even drive them to death.

For Lovers: -

This is an unfavourable period as even very small issues will flare up as big problems leading break up in love. Their love affairs may turn out to be illegal marriages or registered marriages hurting many close relatives and friends. Love affairs will affect education/studies.

Those who are casual in their attitude will get new lovers/beaus causing a hurdle/hiccup in old love affairs leading to break up.

Family results: -

Had there been the association/conjunction of Mercury, Mars, Venus or Mercury, Venus, Moon, in the natal chart the transit of Ketu over Mercury will bring problems/confusion/misunderstandings in the family due to the entry of a third party.

General: -

Transit of Ketu over natal (birth) Mercury will cause problems in the significators of Mercury. There will be mental disturbances, torture, skin-related problems and misunderstandings with friends will crop up.

Encumbered properties will bring litigation and legal remedies has to be sought to solve the problems.

There may be problems by standing guarantee for somebody and if that happens to be the transit of Saturn in the 8th house or Jupiter in the 1st house, the intensity of the problem will multiply compelling repayment of the entire loan money by self/the native.

Lending bankers will press for the repayment of the loan borrowed if any loan is taken from the bank.

Many people will be addicted to intoxication and drugs of different kinds. Some people will indulge in alchemy to make big money and end up with difficulties.

The karaka relations indicated by Mercury like younger sisters, sisters of wives, and very affectionate women will part ways and this will happen if it is the Maha Dasha (Dasha), and Antar Dasha (Bukthi) of Mercury/Ketu or that of planets associated with 1st, 2nd, or 8th house.

Employees/Job workers/artisans/labourers: -

It will be a problematic period for those who are working in registration offices, banks, writers, auditors, typists, and maths teachers and it will be a little less for bank employees.

Role of Mercury in missing/disappearance of articles/persons: -

Mentally retarded people should be well taken care of during this transit period as they may go missing or meet with accidental death.

Similarly, people who are in love should be careful as they may go missing or commit suicide during this transit under extreme circumstances.

Transit of Ketu over natal (birth) Jupiter: -

It is a transit of a yearly planet over another yearly natal planet. The impact of the transit will be more had this been the Maha Dasha (Dasha), or Antar Dasha (Bukthi) of Jupiter/Ketu.

As this is the transit of the planet of wisdom over that of a spiritual planet, it will guide the native to take a devotional/spiritual means to attain wisdom by meditation, penance, holy pilgrimage, and salvation to attain fruitful results.

Those who stayed away from their native place will visit their native places.

There may be abortion in the case of female natives and children may face mental stress. There may be problems in begetting progeny. The Treatment taken for generative sperm cell (spermatorrhoea) growth will fetch fruitful results as there will be conception.

Unremunerative/deteriorated actions are not hindered during the transit of Ketu over natal (birth) Jupiter.

A father had three sons. He undertook holy travel to Varanasi with his third son. Though He had more than 10 family members, why he chose his third son to go with him?

The father had transit Ketu passing over his natal (birth) Jupiter and for his third son transit Jupiter was passing over his natal (birth) Ketu. As Ketu refers to spirituality and holy tours/pilgrimage, the duo undertook a spiritual tour to Varanasi.

If natal (birth) Jupiter and Ketu are very close in degrees and the transit of similar closeness of Jupiter and Ketu will cause undescribed problems and if this happens to be the Maha Dasha (Dasha), or Antar Dasha (Bukthi) of Jupiter/Ketu, the difficulties arise during the transit will be more.

Example: –

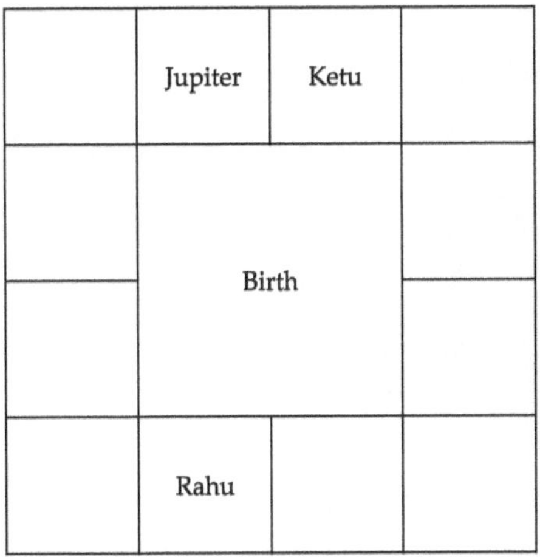

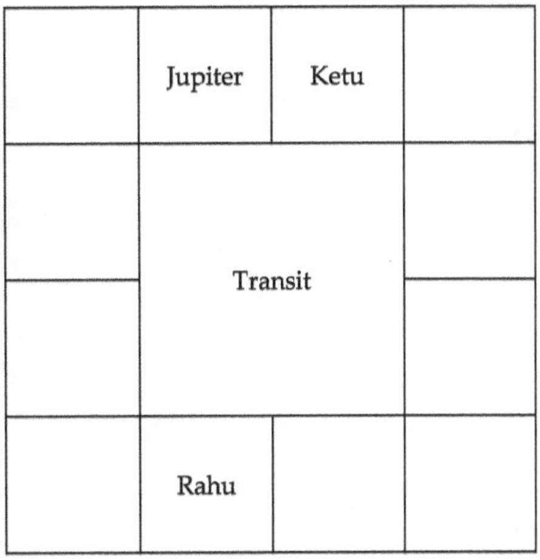

	Jupiter	Ketu				Jupiter	Ketu	
	Birth					Transit		
	Rahu					Rahu		

In the above natal (birth) chart, Jupiter is placed at 10° in Aries, and Ketu is placed at 16° in Taurus separating them both by 36°.

During the transit of Jupiter at 7° in Aries and Ketu at 18° in Taurus bringing them close to their natal placements, the native met with an accident and was affected in the intestine.

This transit reveals the fact that the natives are attacked with sharp weapons, suffer wounds by sharp materials or meet with an accident caused by sharp-edged tools/objects.

The native's friend who had a similar combination of planets was stabbed with a knife. Though no life threat to him, he underwent surgery and had 14 stitches in the stomach. (Ketu refers to stitches).

Example: –

<table>
<tr><td></td><td colspan="2" rowspan="2">Birth</td><td>Rahu</td><td></td><td colspan="2" rowspan="2">Transit</td><td>Rahu</td></tr>
<tr><td rowspan="2">Ketu</td><td rowspan="2"></td><td rowspan="2">Ketu</td><td></td></tr>
<tr><td></td><td>Jupiter</td><td></td><td></td><td></td></tr>
</table>

The above native met with an accident when Jupiter came closer during transit and got affected in the intestine. As there was swelling in his lever, it led to inflammation in his legs giving life threats. He suffered from intestine and liver-related diseases and died without responding to the treatment in ICU.

Example: –

In the below given natal (birth) chart, Jupiter is posited at 213° and Ketu at 119° standing 94° from each other. During the close transit of Jupiter and Ketu, he was working in a poultry farm spraying insecticides over chickens. He was intoxicated by the spray in the intestine and suffered liver-related diseases.

<table>
<tr><td></td><td></td><td></td><td></td></tr>
<tr><td rowspan="2">Rahu
289°</td><td colspan="2" rowspan="2">Birth</td><td>Ketu
119°</td></tr>
<tr><td></td></tr>
<tr><td></td><td>Jupiter
213°</td><td></td><td></td></tr>
</table>

<table>
<tr><td></td><td></td><td>Rahu</td><td></td></tr>
<tr><td rowspan="2"></td><td colspan="2" rowspan="2">Transit</td><td>Jupiter</td></tr>
<tr><td></td></tr>
<tr><td></td><td>Ketu</td><td></td><td></td></tr>
</table>

Due to liver dysfunctions, the level of ammonia increases, and the disease becomes complicated. At last, swelling in the liver and leg portions forced him to fight for life but succumbed to death in the end.

When he died, his wife was four months pregnant and he died before the birth of the child. The transit of Jupiter and Ketu and its related Maha Dasha (Dasha) and Antar Dasha (Bukthi) is the main cause of death.

Transit of Ketu over natal (birth) Venus: –

This refers to the transit of the separator of marital life, Ketu over the Kalathra (Responsible for Marriages) Karaka Venus which is not good as only confusion will prevail duly increasing the problems.

This period should be feared by married people and those who own ancestral properties and are born with female siblings. This transit of a year and a half will harm without fail.

The combination of Venus + Ketu is known as 'Pashandi Yoga/fortune' and those with this sort of planetary combination in their natal (birth) chart will threaten to commit suicide or consume poison even for a very silly problem. My father used to quote about this which was not disputed by 95% of the people.

The transiting Ketu is inimical to natal (birth) Venus causing the worst impact and had this been the Maha Dasha (Dasha), or Antar Dasha (Bukthi) of Venus/Ketu it will flare up the bad results.

For those with Venus + Ketu association in the natal (birth) chart, the transit of Ketu over them will be a horrible period as it will cause separation within the family.

If there are any planets posited in low degrees or high degrees in the houses Taurus or Libra belonging to Venus, then Ketu's transit approach towards Venus will hurt the karaka body parts of that planet.

Had this been the Maha Dasha (Dasha) or Antar Dasha (Bukthi) of the planet posited in the houses Taurus and Libra of Venus are connected with the nodes Rahu/Ketu, the hard impact will be more.

Example:

	Venus (Krittika)		
Rahu	Birth		Ketu (Uthra Phal-guni)
			Ascen-dant

	Ketu		
	Transit		
		Rahu	

For this male native with Virgo ascendant, Venus is posited in Kritika star 1st part and 8th house, Aries and Ketu are in its trine Leo U.Phalguni 1st part. He is certain to face difficulties during the transit of Ketu over natal Venus.

Transit Ketu will not harm the native in his 1st cycle as it is posited in trines to natal Venus and even if he does the impact will not be highly felt by the native.

The transit of Ketu during his 2nd cycle will cause problems. During the transit of Ketu over natal Venus, his wife filed a case against him for dowry harassment and he was arrested in that case. The native was running Venus Maha Dasha (Dasha) and transit Ketu was passing over his 8th house natal Venus confirming it as a case of dowry harassment case which was near fatal. The house in which the transit takes place and the relevant Maha Dasha (Dasha) should be taken into account while considering the impact of the transit of planets.

Example: -

<table>
<tr><td></td><td></td><td></td><td></td><td></td><td></td><td></td><td></td></tr>
<tr><td>Rahu
301°</td><td rowspan="2" colspan="2">Birth</td><td>Venus
119°</td><td>Rahu
321°</td><td rowspan="2" colspan="2">Transit</td><td></td></tr>
<tr><td>Ascen-
dant</td><td>Ketu
121°
Mercury
136°</td><td></td><td>Ketu
141°</td></tr>
<tr><td></td><td></td><td></td><td></td><td></td><td></td><td></td><td></td></tr>
</table>

For this Capricorn ascendant native, Ketu and Mercury are in the 8th house Leo and Venus are posited in the 7th house Cancer. Though the signs in Ketu and Venus posited are different, they are very close degree-wise, which is just 3°.

During the transit of Ketu over natal (birth) Mercury, the native's wife immolated herself using Kerosene, and based on that complaint, the native was arrested.

Here comes the question as to how Venus is affected during the transit of Ketu over natal (birth) Mercury. The answer is the placement of Venus in the asterism Aslesha of Mercury and Mercury in Poorva Phalguna, the star belonging to Venus – an interchange of planets in stars. This facilitated the affliction to Venus instead of Mercury during the transit of Ketu over Mercury.

The above statement reiterates the fact that the interchange of asterisms (stars) should be considered carefully as it alters the result reckoned. Now after the interchange, Venus moves over to the 8th position, indicating the problems through wife, the kalathra karaka Venus and the transit of Ketu over natal Ketu, Venus transpired the case as lethal. The house in which the transit takes place and the relevant Maha Dasha (Dasha) should be taken into account while considering the impact of the transit of planets.

Why did the native's wife immolate herself?

Here Kerosene is considered as watery/liquid and fire as fiery. The transition of stars from watery Cancer to fiery Leo indicates the participation of signs through their respective characteristics. As the interchange is between the asterisms, the real reason behind the immolation is not explicit.

Let us look at the transit and the currency of the Maha Dasha (Dasha), and Antar Dasha (Bukthi) in operation. For Capricorn ascendant, the native was running the 7th and 8th house planets Maha Dasha (Dasha), and Antar Dasha namely Ketu Maha Dasha (Dasha), Mercury Antar Dasha (Bukthi), and Venus Prithy Antar Dasha (Anthram).

It can be noted that the combined planetary positions accounted for the transit and Maha Dasha, Antar Dasha in executing the event so precisely and I pray the Almighty to bestow this knowledge of understanding to human beings.

Note: –

The interchange of signs/houses of the zodiac will explicitly convey problems whereas the interchange of asterisms will not point at problems so explicitly but both will execute the problems with the same intensity.

Transit of Ketu over natal (birth) Saturn: –

The transiting planet is inimical to the natal (birth) planet which will cause a bad impact and had this been the Maha Dasha (Dasha), and Antar Dasha (Bukthi) of Saturn or Ketu the impact will be severe.

The job/work/business will be hindered and that will be based on the lord-ship of Saturn to the ascendant and based on the currency of the Maha Dasha (Dasha) and Antar Dasha (Bukthi).

When the lordship is considered corresponding Maha Dash, Antar Dasha (Bukthi) should be reckoned.

The debt burden will increase for many and they will have mental stress and financial crisis.

Those who are engaged in partnership business have more chances of facing problems forcing them to break the partnership.

This transit will bring problems to those who financially assisted others.

They need not go in search of problems as problems will haunt them.

Saturn is responsible for earning revenue and Ketu prevents income earning and their association and transit are problematic.

Saturn is half-hermit in character and Ketu assumes the nature of an unassumed saint devoid of worldly pleasures. The association of Saturn and Ketu drives us to accept asceticism. Many people look for retirement after handing over their responsibilities to others.

Transit of Ketu over Saturn who is posited alone...

As both are yearly planets, they bring in lifestyle changes.

Transit of Ketu over Saturn associated with the Sun...

It will affect the administration in the business/profession and there will be obstruction/crisis in the business/Profession. In a family business where father and son are involved, it will create problems for both of them. The problems between the administration/management and employees/labourers will emerge.

Transit of Ketu over Saturn associated with the Moon...

This is the transit over the association of a fast-moving planet and a slow-moving planet which leads to mental stress, discomforts/ health issues in the body, losing concentration in the business/ profession, migrating from hometown unable to face the problems in the business/profession, suicidal tendency, and committing suicide. A death in the family causes isolation of family members and it impacts women more than men.

Transit of Ketu over Saturn associated with Mars...

As this transit is over two inimical planets, accidents are caused necessitating surgery. Mechanical professionals/engineers/ industrial business people look for expansion in their field. The aspect of Jupiter will support their efforts and in the absence of Jupiter's aspect, it is better to run the show with existing infrastructure.

Ketu supports unilaterally the business/profession engaged in its karakathuva for example, knitting, thread stores, pooja stores, textile mills, tailoring, wiring, etc.,

Transit of Ketu over Saturn associated with Mercury...

Opportunities to buy a house/land will ensue along with encumbrance and litigation. In the absence of encumbrance/ litigation, the purpose for which the house/land was purchased will not get fulfilled.

Newly married couples will face health issues. Gents will face nervous debility. Diseases like Rheumatism and gas troubles will trouble the native. Legal issues will emerge in already finished jobs.

Transit Ketu over Saturn associated with Venus...

Financial arrangements for business improvement will take a hit and cause a crisis in the business. Legal actions to get the release of funds will fructify during the aspect of Jupiter.

Transit of Ketu over Saturn associated with Rahu/Ketu...

This transit will resemble dying alive as it will cause an internal fear of falling from a height even when securely placed. Many have fallen from high positions during this transit at have struggled long to stage a comeback. It will cause a death in the family in case of a lethal Maha Dasha (Dasha), and Antar Dasha (Bukthi).

Transit of Ketu over Saturn associated with Mandi...

Had this transit period been the death inflicting Maha Dasha (Dasha), Antar Dasha (Bukthi) death of an aged family member will occur or the native will be responsible for a sad incident.

Example 1: -

Birth chart

		Saturn Moon	
	Birth		

Transit chart

			Ketu
	Transit		
	Rahu		

In the above natal (birth) chart, the Moon and Saturn are conjoined in Mercury's Gemini sign. The Moon is posited in the star Mrigasira of death inflicting planet Mars and Saturn is in the Arudra star of Rahu. This native was running Mars Maha Dasha during the transit of Ketu over Saturn + Moon combination and for Gemini ascendant Mars Maha Dasha inflicts death.

This native was affected by a mental disorder when Ketu approached natal (birth) Saturn in Gemini. The disease started to become severe with Ketu getting closer and closer to the Moon prompting treatment under care in ICU. The native did not how he survived till the completion of the transit as in this planetary combination Ketu inflicts death or near-death sequences.

Another person had a similar planetary combination in his natal (birth) chart, but he was not running death-inflicting Maha Dasha. He suffered a big financial crisis and could not sleep for a year without sleeping doses.

The increased dosage of sleeping tablets rendered him sleepless and he recovered from it after a great struggle. This transit affects business people and enlightens business wisdom in them.

		Saturn	
Jupiter	Birth		
	Example 2		

		Moon Saturn	Ketu
	Birth		
	Example 3		
Rahu		Mars	

Example 2: –

Transit Ketu is passing over natal (birth) Saturn and this native experienced business hurdles. He borrowed a little to overcome his financial problems in the business. As his Saturn received the aspect of natal Jupiter, he could overcome his problems and get relieved after the transit.

Example 3: -

In this case, transit Ketu is moving towards the Moon + Saturn combination which is under the 8th aspect of natal (birth) Mars causing difficulties in business.

He borrowed heavily beyond his capacity to overcome the difficulties but he could not withstand the problems and realized that his life is beyond recovery.

Reason: -

Transit Ketu acquired more strength from natal Ketu in Gemini while moving from Gemini to Taurus causing more crisis to the native.

At times sub-rules play more effective roles than principal rules and an analysis of the transit positions from all angles will be an ideal solution.

Transit of Ketu in Taurus

<table>
<tr><td></td><td></td><td>Saturn</td><td></td></tr>
<tr><td></td><td rowspan="2" colspan="2" align="center">Birth
Example 4</td><td></td></tr>
<tr><td></td><td></td></tr>
<tr><td></td><td></td><td></td><td></td></tr>
</table>

<table>
<tr><td></td><td></td><td>Saturn
Jupiter</td><td></td></tr>
<tr><td></td><td rowspan="2" colspan="2" align="center">Birth
Example 5</td><td></td></tr>
<tr><td></td><td></td></tr>
<tr><td></td><td></td><td></td><td></td></tr>
</table>

Example 4: -

Transit Ketu is passing over natal (birth) Saturn. He had some difficulties in his business and to set it right he borrowed some money. He struggled and overcame the difficulty.

Example 5: –

In this case, Ketu is transiting over natal (birth) Saturn and Jupiter in Taurus forcing him to struggle in business. He borrowed beyond his capacity and entangled in an irrecoverable position in life as the planet supporting recovery Jupiter is also in the web.

He suffered rheumatism as transit Ketu conjoined Jupiter and Saturn. His liver got damaged and was suffering in his old age unable to take rest due to over-commitments.

Transit Rahu/Ketu over natal (birth) Rahu/Ketu...

It is the transit movement in the opposite direction to the natal placement which has pushed many natives to their unimaginable bottom positions.

Those who faded out of their life after a salient living were subjected during the transit of Ketu with the lords of death inflicting, 8th, and inimical/evil positions.

This impact is dependent on the capacity of the native.

An astrologer can reveal all types of difficulties/problems that a human can face in life to the native who will accept without any objection.

If this transit period happens to be the Maha Dasha (Dasha), or Antar Dasha (Bukthi) of death-inflicting, inimical/evil, or that of the 8th lord or that of Rahu/Ketu/Saturn, then the impact will be enormous, magnifying the existing problems and pushing towards death or near-death situations.

Though natal (birth) Rahu/Ketu does some good, it will never do any good during its transit. It may seem to elevate, but ultimately it will ditch to an unknown level. The transit supports patients' recovery.

The transit will separate people close to the heart by creating misunderstanding. It will cause unending enmity, unpayable loans, and unending sorrow.

If Rahu/Ketu finds no planets in the sign in which they are moving from one sign to the other, the native will not be impacted or gets no benefit.

Transit planets change the attitude/character of a native while the Maha Dasha (Dasha), Antar Dasha (Bukthi), and Prithyantar Dasha (Anthram) cause an event to the native.

In the case of two friends, the transit of Saturn was over natal (birth) Rahu for one and Ketu was transiting over natal (birth) Saturn for the other. Both were doing business individually for more than four years. Person 1 had business hurdles and crises impacting not only business but also those around him including his friend, the 2nd person who helped him financially. The 2nd person's money that was given to his friend got blocked during the transit of Ketu over his natal (birth) Saturn and he was pushed to an unrecoverable position.

Person 2 was running Ketu Maha Dasha (Dasha), Ketu Antar Dasha (Bukthi), and Saturn Prithyantar Dasha (Anthram) which aggravated the impact of the transit forcing him to attempt suicide which affected his health.

As the lord of evil (Bhadagathipathi) Mars threw his aspect on Saturn increasing the tussle between already existing between Saturn and Ketu.

The transiting planet is inimical to the natal (birth) planet. Had this been the Maha Dasha (Dasha), Antar Dasha (Bukthi) of Saturn, or Ketu, the impact will be more.

The transit will separate people close to the heart by creating misunderstanding. It will cause unending enmity, unpayable loans, and unending sorrow.

Transit of Ketu over natal (birth) Ketu...

The transiting planet is inimical to the natal (birth) planet. Had this been the Maha Dasha (Dasha), Antar Dasha (Bukthi) of Saturn, or Ketu, the impact will be more.

The natal (birth) Rahu will do good but not transit Rahu.

If Rahu/Ketu finds no planets in the sign in which they are moving from one sign to the other, the native will not be impacted or gets no benefit. If the planet posited there is currently running the

Maha Dasha (Dasha) or Antar Dasha (Bukthi) their indication of malefic bhavas causes malefic results.

If Rahu/Ketu finds no planets in the sign in which they are moving from one sign to the other, the native will not be impacted or gets no benefit. The transiting Rahu/Ketu impact planets posited in the asterism, its 10th as well as 19th asterism

The transit will separate people close to the heart by creating misunderstanding. It will cause unending enmity, unpayable loans, and unending sorrow.

Transit of Ketu over natal (birth) Saturn: -

The transiting planet is inimical to the natal (birth) planet. The native was running Saturn Maha Dasha (Dasha), Mercury Antar Dasha (Bukthi), and Ketu Prithyantar Dasha (Anthram) during which he experienced severe business crises which is beyond mentioning and it touched the zenith during Ketu prityantar Dasha. The transit of the planet of wisdom over the karmic planet induces spiritual energy.

The combination/association of Saturn + Ketu + Jupiter inflicts death, cripples the activities of the native, and causes laziness. The native may have revenue dues that will not be forthcoming causing business problems.

Transiting Ketu over the natal (birth) Saturn having Jupiter's connection indicates death and if the current Maha Dasha (Dasha) lord is linked to this it causes death or near-death situations.

It causes paralysis to many and impounds them. Only when the Maha Dasha (Dasha) lord is connected with Saturn and Ketu, death occurs.

In the absence of any connection to Saturn to Ketu Maha Dasha (Dasha) or Antar Dasha (Bukthi) or Prityantar Dasha (Anthram) wise during the currency of this transit, the results are not so vulnerable but fear about the profession/business prevailed.

26.

MANTHI

Sun + Manthi: -

Implies lethality to paternal side, blemishes, and curses present. It indicates the blemish descended from ancestral genre and prevention from enjoying the benefits from ancestral properties. It brings disgrace in own community/group.

Moon + Manthi: -

Indicates lethality on the maternal side, blemishes, and curses present. It implies the blemish descended from the mother's side genre and separation amongst the relations, mental fears, and sudden mental aberrations.

Mars + Manthi: -

Blood-related lethal implications, blemishes, blemish impact on siblings, and curses present. It causes diseases and enmity.

Mercury + Manthi: -

Lethal implications to maternal uncles, blemishes, and curses are shown by this combination. The native will be impacted by the curses/blemishes of spinsters/unmarried women and will lack grasping.

Jupiter + Manthi: -

Genetic lethality, blemishes, and progenitor curses are indicated by this combination. This will affect the children.

The native will not get a good preceptor and will not beget the desired children. Even when desired children are born, they will choose their life path.

Venus + Manthi: -

Blemishes through women, curses of women, women inherited blemishes will haunt the native. It shows the blemish, and lethality through the wife.

Saturn + Manthi: -

It indicates the strong curse/blemish of family/tutelary deities. It strongly indicates unfulfilled offerings/submissions to family/ tutelary deities. The native will not have good servants/sub-ordinates/employees and will not get any job/income that is worth his knowledge/education/capabilities. This placement causes separation within relations and mental and startling fear.

Rahu + Manthi: -

Lethality, blemishes, and curses drawn from forefathers of the paternal side are indicated. The native will fear poisoning/ intoxication. Disgrace, humiliation, and loss will chase the native. Big mortality will horrify the native.

Ketu + Manthi: -

Lethality, blemishes, and curses drawn from forefathers of the maternal side are indicated. The native will fear poisoning/ intoxication. Disgrace, humiliation, and loss will chase the native. The native will face separation and legal cases and will receive punishment.

Ascendant + Manthi: -

There will be life threats to the natives and lethal situations will appear before sight.

Whichever planet travels over Manthi, leads to death.

The transit Moon over natal (birth) Manthi exposes the mental status of the native and the incidents that have happened or are about to happen. The native for whom the transit Moon is passing over the natal (birth) Manthi hears about the death of a person.

Transit of Saturn over natal (birth) Sun…

<table>
<tr><td></td><td>Saturn</td><td></td></tr>
<tr><td rowspan="2"></td><td rowspan="2">Birth
1st Son</td><td></td><td></td></tr>
<tr><td>Sun</td></tr>
<tr><td></td><td></td><td></td><td></td></tr>
</table>

<table>
<tr><td></td><td></td><td>Saturn</td><td></td></tr>
<tr><td>Sun</td><td rowspan="2">Birth
2nd Son</td><td></td></tr>
<tr><td></td><td></td></tr>
<tr><td></td><td></td><td></td><td></td></tr>
</table>

<table>
<tr><td></td><td></td><td></td><td></td></tr>
<tr><td rowspan="2"></td><td rowspan="2">Birth
3rd Sun</td><td>Saturn</td><td></td></tr>
<tr><td></td></tr>
<tr><td></td><td>Sun</td><td></td><td></td></tr>
</table>

<table>
<tr><td></td><td></td><td>Sun</td><td></td></tr>
<tr><td rowspan="2"></td><td rowspan="2">Transit
Death of the Father</td><td></td></tr>
<tr><td>Saturn</td></tr>
<tr><td></td><td></td><td></td><td></td></tr>
</table>

The above native experienced 3 incidents.

1. His father died.
2. He was punished by his superiors.
3. He suffered from diabetes.

This transit draws so much vulnerability because the transit Sun is passing over natal (birth) Saturn and the transit Saturn is moving over the natal (birth) Sun stressing the impact of this double transit. He has three sons.

These three incidents in some way should be correlated with his sons' natal chart which is as under.

His father died when transit Saturn was passing over the natal (birth) Sun in his **First (native)** son's natal chart.

At the same time, in **the Second** son's natal chart, the transit Saturn threw its aspect on the natal (birth) Sun and the natal (birth) Saturn.

It was also the period during which the transit Saturn threw its aspect on the natal (birth) Sun in his **third** son's natal chart.

His father-in-law died when the transit Saturn and transit Sun were passing over the natal (birth) Sun in his **third** son's natal chart.

The First son (the native) was very affectionate towards his father and hence the dual transit perfectly matched with the father's death and concurred with his natal chart. His second son parted from his father and was living separately.

His third son was attached to his in-laws and his natal chart defined those relating to his father-in-law as he was not in touch with his father. His native chart did not reveal anything about his father's death which proves that the natal chart reveals the good or bad facts only about whom the native is attached to.

Acquisition of a house…

A person wants to construct a house. How to answer him? What are the planetary placements for this?

Mars + Moon

Mars + Venus

Mars + Jupiter

The above three combinations are connections responsible for the acquisition of a house.

Mars + Moon combination induces the thoughts and efforts to construct a house.

Mars + Venus combination presses the need to construct a house for the future or to keep the prestige.

Mars + Jupiter combination indicates the circumstantial acquisition of house property by virtues.

Which transit period will support the acquisition of a house: -

When the aspect of transit Jupiter or Venus falls on the 4th house or 4th bhava a native acquires a house.

While Mars transits over natal (birth) Jupiter or Jupiter transits over natal (birth) Mars a native acquires a house.

A House property is a long-lasting one and hence the support of Maha Dasha (Dasha) and Antar Dasha is essential to acquire one. The Maha Dasha (Dasha), and Antar Dasha (Bukthi) of the 4th house and 11th houses should be in operation or it may be that of the 2nd and 11th houses.

27.

RESULTS BY RETROGRADE PLANETS ON THEIR RETURN

Transit planets induce the native to do an action during their direct transit over a natal (birth) planet. The transiting planet gives sufficient time for the action to materialize during its direct transit. When the native does not make use of the time given, the transiting planet magnifies the event and gives good or bad results when it retrogrades.

The results, good or bad occur depending upon the significators of the bhava and planets associated, conjoined, combined or aspect of the planet.

Example: -

		Ascen-dant Jupiter 12.30°	
	Female Chart		

		→ Jupiter ←	
	Transit		

For the above Taurus ascendant native female, 8th lord Jupiter is in the ascendant at 12.30 degrees and transit Jupiter is passing over Taurus. The native started experiencing problems of insult and sorrow when transit Jupiter approached 11.45 degrees and it seem to subsidise at 16 degrees.

The transit Jupiter after touching 16 degrees retrograded and returned only to aggravate the humiliation already suffered and the native's family suffered humiliation when transit Jupiter touched natal (birth) Jupiter at 12 degrees.

The event: -

The female native eloped with her lover when transit Jupiter touched the natal (birth) Jupiter on its onward march but was caught by her parents and relatives in just two hours. She remained silent and behaved well till Jupiter touched 16 degrees. Believing her character her marriage was fixed with another person. Two days before the marriage, she eloped again with her lover when transit retrograde Jupiter touched the natal (birth) Jupiter. Now Jupiter on its retrograde motion gave humiliation and waste of money.

Notes: -

Such is the power of the transiting planets who cautions during their direct motion over malefic attributable planets and aggravates the actions on their return in retrograde motion exhibiting the impact of people who eloped, thieves and those who have not refrained their first grievous actions.

This reverses to good results like getting the old dues back, an asset presumed as lost coming back in good form happens during the transit over the planets of benefic significators.

Natal planets in 1 – 7 samasaptak position: -

Planets posited in 1 – 7 positions to each other known as 'samasaptaka' will get affected by the transit of Rahu/Ketu. An event that is about to happen due to the placements of natal (birth) planets will increase depending upon the bhava significators of the planets associated with or aspect of it.

Retrograde planets and Rahu/Ketu in transit: -

If Rahu/Ketu in transit approach a planet that is in retrograde motion, it conveys beneficial results to the native and the quantum of the benefit depends on the planets associated, combined, conjoined or aspect the planet and its bhava significators.

Example: -

			Saturn				Ketu
	Birth				Transit		
Moon				Rahu			

It is to be seen from the above natal (birth) chart that Rahu/Ketu transit affects the planets in the 1 – 7 samasaptak axis.

This transit may appear to enhance/elevate the status of the native but will hinder for real. The native may either escape from the hurdles or manage the situation.

Business/profession, the mental status will stutter which is t a yoga. At times this interchange of houses by the Moon and Saturn proves to be fatal.

The interchange of houses by the Moon and Saturn will not confer the significators based on the ascendant and karaka.

Example: -

		Saturn					Ketu	
		Birth						
	Jupiter					Rahu		

It is to be seen from the above natal (birth) chart that Rahu/Ketu transit affects the planets in 1 – 7 namely Jupiter and Saturn samasaptak axis.

This transit may appear to enhance/elevate the status of the native but will hinder for real. The native may either escape from the hurdles or manage the situation.

Business/profession, the mental status will stutter which is t a yoga. At times this interchange of houses between Jupiter and Saturn proves to be fatal.

The interchange of houses by Jupiter and Saturn will not confer the significators based on the ascendant and karaka.

Example: -

		Saturn	
	Birth	Mars	
	Jupiter Venus		

		Ketu	
	Transit		
	Rahu		

It is to be seen from the above natal (birth) chart that Rahu/Ketu transit affects the planets in 1 – 7 namely Jupiter, Venus, and Saturn samasaptak axis.

These three planets confer money, grains, and wealth through their karakathuvas and their affliction by Rahu and Ketu forbids their benefit.

Mars in receipt of the beneficial aspect of Jupiter in its natal (birth) position did not harm on a big scale or lowered its malefic impact during its impact.

Mars gives hard impacts during its transit when it receives the aspect of Saturn in the natal (birth) chart.

Notes: -

Saturn gives hard impacts during its transit when it receives the aspect of Mars in the natal (birth) chart.

Mars afflicted by Rahu in the natal (birth) chart carries the inimical qualities in its transit too. This can be compared to a person with an inherited disease, carrying it throughout life.

A planet in transit exhibits the good or bad qualities it acquired in its natal (birth) position.

Transit and time of event: –

Moon Jupiter	Birth		

		Jupiter (Rohini)	
	Transit		
			Moon (Pooram)

In the natal (birth) chart, Jupiter and Moon are conjoined in Aquarius. This native will experience the Moon + Jupiter planetary combination transit results when Jupiter and Moon pass over their asterisms/stars Rohini, Hastham, Sravana (Thiruvonam), Punarvasu, Purva Vishaka, and Purva Bhadra.

The conjunction or aspect of the Moon during her transit over natal (birth) Jupiter + Moon conveys the transit results. This woman bright disrepute humiliation to her family.

According to the transit at that time…

Jupiter was transiting in the Moon's star Rohini. The Moon's aspect of natal (birth) Jupiter + Moon during its transit in Purva Phalguna (pooram) of Venus, the dispositor of transiting Jupiter activated the event bringing disrepute, disgrace and humiliation to the woman's family.

28.

EXCHANGE OF HOUSES

In the exchange of houses by two planets, both the planets share the good or bad results that they acquire instead of assuming individually.

Escape of a planet from impact due to the exchange of Houses: -

		Saturn				Ketu	
	Birth				Transit		
Mars	Jupiter				Rahu		

Jupiter and Saturn are in the 1 – 7 samasaptak axis. Here Jupiter and Mars exchange their houses which signifies the inheritance of malefic results during the transit of Rahu by mutually shifting to their original houses of Sagittarius and Scorpio.

Or

Mars as natural malefic is impacted more by the transit of Rahu/Ketu instead of Jupiter after an exchange of houses.

29.

EXCHANGE OF HOUSES LEADING TO THE ARREST OF THE FORTUNE OF A PLANET DUE TO GET OR SHARING IT WITH THE OTHER PLANET: -

		Saturn	
	Example 1		
	Example 1		
Mars	Jupiter		

Mars		Saturn	
	Example 2		
	Example 2		
	Jupiter		

Both Jupiter and Saturn are on the 1 – 7 axis. As Jupiter and Mars exchange their houses, the benefits due from the transit of Jupiter will neither be available to Jupiter nor to Mars each giving way for the other to get.

Else…

The benefits due to Jupiter's transit are being shared by both Jupiter and Mars as both are placed in 2/12 positions between them.

In example 2, the benefits due to Jupiter's transit are being shared by both Jupiter and Mars as both are placed in 5/9 positions between them.

Correlation of Bhava and Karaka

Birth 1

Ascendant Mars			
		Venus	

Birth 2

Mars			Venus
Ascendant			

It is a general rule that the marital life will not be blissful when the Kalathra (spouse indicators) Karakas Mars and Venus are afflicted by Rahu and Ketu but the reason for such denial should be reckoned from the bhava where the Kalathra Karakas are posited.

In both birth charts, Mars and Venus are in Aquarius and Leo. Rahu is transiting in Aquarius and Venus is transiting in Leo.

In birth chart 1, the native who had Mars and Venus in the 1 – 7 axis faced marital separation.

For the person in chart 2, it gave deficiency in libido triggering the 3rd house.

By this, it has to be assessed through which bhava the karakathuvas will be affected.

30.

COMBUSTION

Planets that are very close to the Sun suffer combustion and extend only combusted results in whichever sign they are posited in.

The position of Mars, Mercury, Jupiter, Saturn, and Venus within of° to the Sun is considered as combustion as per combustion rules. But I consider reckoning combustion within 5° close to the Sun.

Results of combustion: -

A natal (birth) combusted planet loses its total significators and extends only malefic results.

But it gives 25% of its karakathuva results. Hence combusted planets deny or lower the quantum of the benefits they are supposed to give.

Along with the Dig Bala, Kala Bala, cheshta Bala, Ayana Bala, Putch Bala, and Sthana Bala of a planet, its position in the Graha yudh should be weighed before declaring the transit relates as it will enhance its quality. Hence, I reiterate the need to have thorough knowledge about the transit concerning all areas.

Example: –

<table>
<tr><td></td><td></td><td></td><td></td><td style="border:none;width:40px"></td><td></td><td></td><td></td><td></td></tr>
<tr><td rowspan="2"></td><td colspan="3" rowspan="2" align="center">Birth</td><td></td><td style="border:none"></td><td rowspan="2"></td><td colspan="3" rowspan="2" align="center">Transit</td></tr>
<tr><td></td><td style="border:none"></td></tr>
<tr><td>Sun 18°
Jupiter
14°</td><td></td><td></td><td></td><td style="border:none"></td><td>Saturn
10°</td><td></td><td></td></tr>
</table>

In the above natal (birth) chart, The Sun and Jupiter are in Sagittarius and Jupiter is in combustion. Hence Saturn did not give any good or bad results during its transit over natal (birth) Jupiter.

The native could not enjoy any big benefic results during the transit of Saturn over the Sun and Jupiter for two reasons.

1. The combust Jupiter can gain no power or benefits from any planet.
2. Jupiter's combust position with the Sun pushes the transit Saturn also in a combust conjunction preventing any good benefic results to the native.

When the transit benefits of a planet over a natal planet are exhibited, it has to be assessed from the weightage of the planets for non-delivery of the benefits.

Example: –

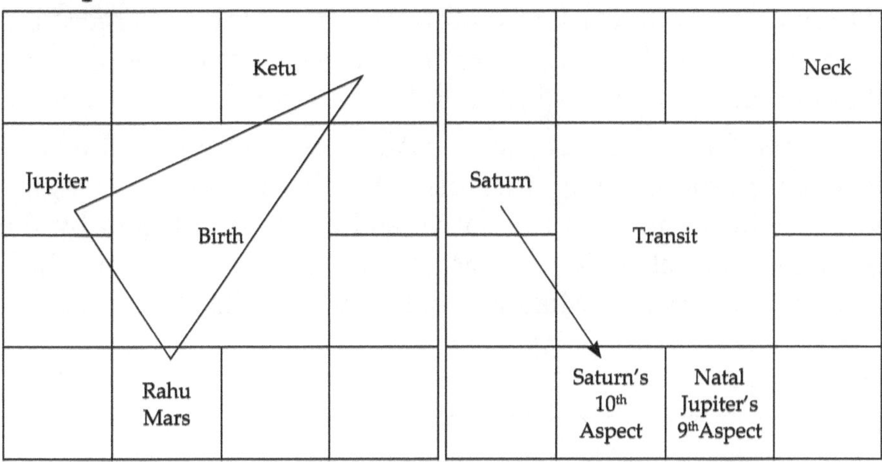

Jupiter is in Aquarius and Rahu + Mars are closely placed in Scorpio. The 4th aspect of Mars is on Jupiter preventing the benefits conferred by the friendly planets of Jupiter while passing over Jupiter.

The native of the above natal (birth) chart could not get the benefits to be conferred by the transiting Saturn over Jupiter and those given partly were that of the Karagathuvas of Mars and Rahu. He bought a house under hypothecation and land through instalments.

During the same time, he met with an accident and was hospitalised for a few weeks due to the combined aspect of Rahu and Mars over transit Saturn. Later he suffered from a stiff neck, the karaka of the Gemini sign due to the combined aspect of Rahu and Mars along with that of Jupiter who received the same.

Jupiter is associated with Saturn which is responsible for contraction, epilepsy, sprain, and flatulence (gas problems). As Jupiter has acquired the characteristics of Saturn and the combined characteristics of Rahu + Mars, its aspect of the Gemini sign caused stiffness in the neck.

During the transit of Saturn in Aquarius, it receives the aspect of natal (birth) Rahu + Mars which it reflects back through its 10th aspect on the natal (birth) Rahu + Mars causing the accident to the native. Depending upon the currency of the Maha Dasha (Dasha), and Antar Dasha (Bukthi) the parts of the body receiving the aspect of natal (birth)Jupiter are affected since Jupiter receives the combined malefic aspect of Rahu + Jupiter.

When Saturn approaches the Aquarius sign where the natal Jupiter is posited, the significators of karaka and bhava belonging to Leo will do good to the native as Leo is not affected by the combined aspect of Rahu + Mars. But the Gemini sign which receives the aspect of Mars will deter the benefits to the native.

Example: –

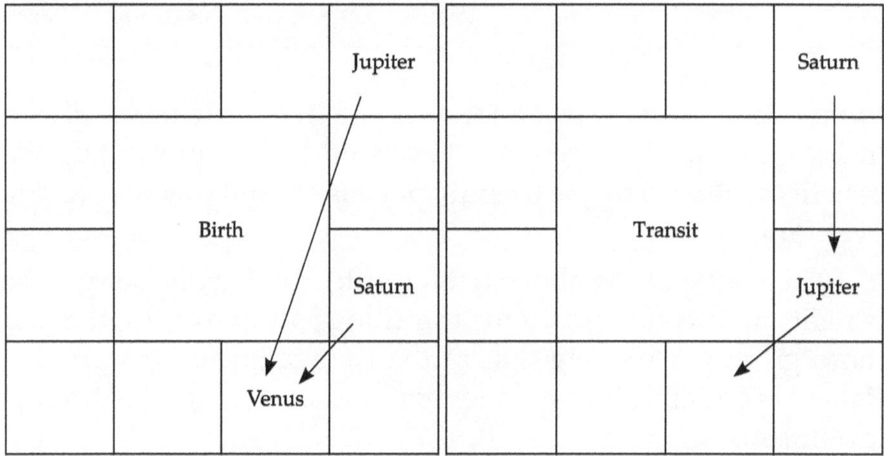

Jupiter is in Gemini and Saturn is in Leo. Venus in Libra receives the 5th aspect of Jupiter and the 3rd aspect of Saturn conferring beneficial results to the native during the transit of friendlier planets over natal (birth) Jupiter and natal (birth) Saturn. (Thus, the friendlier, enmity, aspect and its strength should be considered for arriving at the results).

This native has Venus in Libra under the aspect of Jupiter and Saturn. Saturn conferred supreme beneficial results during its transit in Libra over Venus and enriched the karaka, and bhavagas indicated by Libra. Jupiter + Saturn combination extended their benefits to natal (birth) Venus in the form of Money, grain, and wealth.

The native will gain beneficial results during the transit of Mars, Jupiter, Venus, and Saturn in Gemini and during the transit of Jupiter, Venus, and Saturn in Leo. As Saturn is in 'bhadagasthana' – evil 11th house, the beneficial results through Saturn will be less compared to that of Jupiter.

When one of the two planets in the 1 – 7 samsaptak axis receives the aspect of other planets: -

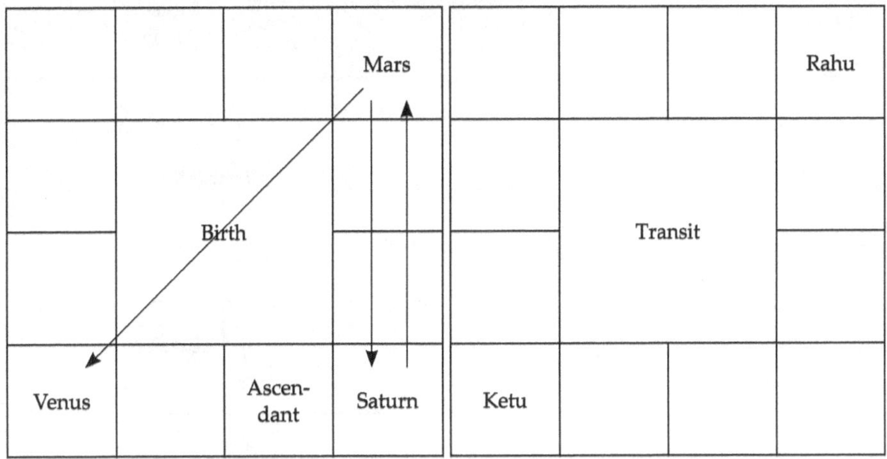

For this native with Libra ascendant, Venus is in Sagittarius and Mars is in Gemini in 1 – 7 samsaptak axis. Mars in Gemini and Saturn in Virgo get the mutual aspect by the 4th and 10th.

As both the Kalathra (marriage significators) karaka lords Mars and Venus were afflicted by Rahu and Ketu simultaneously, according to our rules of affliction to marital life, the couple got separated.

To know the cause behind their separation, the bhava occupied by the Kalathra lords should be considered. As they are in the 3rd bhava to Libra ascendant, suspicion of fidelity and sexual habits lead to the separation.

Notes: -
Venus in the 3rd house instigates suspicion by the husband about the wife and Mars in the 3rd house arouses suspicion about husband to wife.

Mars's aspect of the 3rd bhava with the combined 10th aspect of Saturn over it indicates unusual/abnormal sexual habits. This also indicates the disease signified by the Virgo Saturn receiving the aspect of Rahu afflicted Mars.

Example: –

Mars	Ketu	Moon	Ascendant
	Birth		
		Rahu	

	Mars Venus Ketu	Jupiter Moon	Ascendant
	Transit		
		Saturn Rahu	

In this Gemini ascendant chart, the Moon is in Taurus and Ketu is in Aries.

1) Jupiter is transiting over the Moon in Taurus.
2) Ketu is transiting over natal (birth) Ketu in Aries.

Result: –

When Jupiter was passing over the natal (birth) Moon, the native was subjected to humiliation. During the transit of Ketu over natal (birth) Ketu, his wife eloped from the house.

This transit happened during the currency of Jupiter Maha Dasha (Dasha) bringing humiliation to the native. The first cycle of Jupiter did not bring hard impacts as he was not running Jupiter Maha Dasha (Dasha).

Example: –

		Saturn				Jupiter Ketu	Ascen-dant
Rahu	Birth	Ketu			transit		
Ascen-dant	Jupiter					Rahu	Saturn

During the birth Saturn is in Taurus and Jupiter is in Scorpio. Though the transit of Jupiter in Taurus over natal (birth) Saturn is considered good, Ketu transiting along with Jupiter prevented the benefits discharged by Jupiter. Ketu's transit over natal (birth) Saturn bothers him. Likewise, Rahu is passing over natal (birth) Jupiter indicating that huge money has got blocked. Had this been the currency of the Maha Dasha (Dasha), Antar Dasha (Bukthi) of Jupiter and Saturn combination, the impact will be hard. The bhava indicated by the hegemony of Jupiter and Saturn will be affected.

While the transit simply removes your shirt, transit integrated with Maha Dasha (Dasha), Antar Dasha (Bukthi) will exuviate you (whip you until your skin peels off).

What is the effect of Jupiter's transit over natal (birth) Saturn: -

This native did not feel the pain or the impact as Ketu moved out earlier in the dual transit of Jupiter and Ketu. Jupiter guarded against the odd. Had it been otherwise i.e., the exit of Jupiter first and Ketu thereafter, he would be experiencing the paid even after the transit.

Example: -

Birth

	Birth		
Ascen-dant		Moon Mercury	Mars

Transit

	Mars Ketu	Jupiter	Ascen-dant
	Transit		
		Saturn Rahu	

In the above natal chart, the Moon and Mercury are placed in Libra and transit entered into Libra 1st signifying the **Sade-Sati (Seven-and-a-half-year)** giving unbearable bitter experiences to the native.

Now, Rahu entered into Libra and blew up the bitter scenario causing separation in the family. The younger sister of the native, the karaka of Mercury parted from the family.

Saturn and Rahu in Libra act as two ends of a rope to churn.

This transit caused mental torture and impairment of thoughts. As both planets are feminine in nature, he was hurt by ladies.

When will this be all right?

During the transit of Jupiter in Gemini, its aspect on the natal (birth) Mercury and the Moon will set right the situation or the native will be ready to face the problems.

Stoppage of Income: -

Transit of Rahu/Ketu should be analysed to check the stoppage of income to a native.

Conjunction, association or aspect of inimical planets in transit over Jupiter + Saturn combination will hinder the fortune of income.

If Jupiter + Saturn combine and occupy the evil places 6th, 8th, or 12th house from the ascendant, it hinders the fortune conferred by the Saturn + Jupiter combination.

1. Both ends like, fortunes conferred and evil effects will be in high proportions.
2. This combination need not be feared when Saturn retrograde.
3. When transit Rahu/Ketu pass over natal (birth) Jupiter, Saturn there will be a break in service, hurdles in business, and problems within partners will hinder income.
4. Problems unconnected with the business will pop up.
5. In a few cases, the income will stop before realising/ understanding the problems.
6. Self-prestige will be affected forcing a few to resign from their job.

The transit that affects the income: -

Rule No. 1: -

There will be a stoppage/break in income when Rahu/Ketu transit over the karaka of revenue Jupiter or lord of the 2nd house.

Rule No 2: -

There will be stoppage/hurdles in income from business/ profession when Rahu/Ketu transit over Saturn or lord of the 10th house, the Karaka for profession/business.

Hence to judge the stoppage/hurdles in income from profession/business, the transit of Rahu/Ketu should be examined carefully along with the conjunction/association of the lords of the 4th house, 6th house, or 12th house.

What is the difference between two planets in the same signs and their trines?

Problems will be persistent when two planets are posited in the same sign from the very beginning of the event travelling along. In the case of their placement in trines, the problems will crop up at a later stage.

Rahu gives hurdles and stoppages in a profession/business whereas Ketu causes crises in the business/profession.

Rahu + Ketu: -

When Rahu/Ketu transit over the exact degrees in which natal (birth) Rahu/Ketu are posited, it changes the course of the life or uproots the central axis.

The association of Rahu/Ketu with any planet turns into a blemish-causing unnatural death, many accidents, and horrific incidents, Great fall of reputed corporates, big dynasties, conglomerates and giant industries are during the association of planets with Rahu/Ketu only.

Example: -

<table>
<tr><td></td><td></td><td></td><td></td></tr>
<tr><td rowspan="2">Rahu</td><td rowspan="2" colspan="2">07-07-1953</td><td>Ketu</td></tr>
<tr><td></td></tr>
<tr><td></td><td></td><td>Saturn</td></tr>
</table>

<table>
<tr><td></td><td></td><td></td><td></td></tr>
<tr><td rowspan="2">Rahu</td><td rowspan="2" colspan="2">25-07-1953</td><td>Ketu</td></tr>
<tr><td></td></tr>
<tr><td>Moon</td><td></td><td>Saturn</td></tr>
</table>

In the natal chart, If Saturn initially touches Rahu or Ketu, it indicates that the native will have severe crises in the business/ profession.

The native who is born on 25-07-1953 will face fewer problems than the one born on 07-07-1953 as Transit Saturn meets the Moon before touching Rahu in its trine reducing the impact and indicating relatively fewer problems.

In the first natal (birth) chart, Saturn first touches Rahu directly, but in the next chart touches the Moon in between Saturn and Rahu.

Example: –

Birth chart:

Ascendant Mercury	Ketu		
	Birth		
		Mars	
Saturn	Rahu	Jupiter	

Transit chart:

	Jupiter	Ketu	
	Transit		Moon (Pushya)
	Rahu	Saturn	

In the above natal (birth) chart, Saturn gets the 4th aspect of Mars posited in Scorpio. The native was engaged in the machinery industry, the karaka of Saturn and Mars did not prevent it. He carried on well till the end of Jupiter Maha Dasha (Dasha) to be cheated by his friend in Saturn Maha Dasha (Dasha), and Saturn Antar Dasha (Bukthi).

This Pisces ascendant native approached in April 2012 for consultation and to look at the transit chart on that date.

The native was running Saturn Maha Dasha (Dasha), Saturn Antar Dasha (Bukthi), and Saturn Prithyantar Dasha (Anthram) and the ruling star of the day is Pushya of Saturn compelling the need to focus on the transit of Saturn.

The transit Saturn is passing over natal (birth) Rahu.

Transit Rahu is passing over natal (birth) Saturn.

Transit Jupiter is moving over natal (birth) Ketu.

The above transit is a severe one and will cause near-death situations along with huge loss and Saturn is transiting in the evil 8th house to the Pisces ascendant extending unbearable humiliation.

The native came to know about the deception by his friend the day Rahu began to transit over natal (birth) Saturn and within three hours the problem blew up as the amount cheated stood at a few crores.

During the transit of Saturn over natal (birth) Rahu, those people affected by the cheat have filed a case against the native before a competent authority.

As both natal (birth) Saturn and transit Saturn were in retrograde motion, the impact experienced by the native was under control.

31.

DATES OF JUPITER'S ENTRY INTO A RASI/SIGN

In the below-given Table, the date of entry of Jupiter in a Sign is given. The retrograde motion of Jupiter is not given here. To know the answers to the questions as to When was the earlier transit results by Jupiter? How was it? When will it recur? How will it be? can be known from the table below which is for 24 years.

Rasi/Sign	From	To	From	To
Aries	26.05.1999	02.06.2000	08.05.2011	17.05.2012
Taurus	02.06.2000	08.05.2001	17.05.2012	31.05.2013
Gemini	08.05.2001	05.07.2002	31.05.2013	19.06.2014
Cancer	05.07.2002	30.07.2003	19.06.2014	14.07.2015
Leo	30.07.2003	27.08.2004	14.07.2015	11.08.2016
Virgo	27.08.2004	28.09.2005	11.08.2016	12.09.2017
Libra	28.09.2005	27.10.2006	12.09.2017	11.10.2018
Scorpio	27.10.2006	27.11.2007	11.10.2018	04.11.2019
Sagittarius	27.11.2007	09.12.2008	04.11.2019	20.11.2020
Capricorn	09.12.2008	01.05.2009	20.11.2020	20.11.2021
Aquarius	01.05.2009	02.05.2010	20.11.2021	13.04.2022
Pisces	02.05.2010	08.05.2011	13.04.2022	22.04.2023

32.

DATES OF SATURN'S ENTRY INTO A RASI/SIGN

In the below-given Table, the date of entry of Saturn in a Sign is given. The retrograde motion of Saturn is not given here. To know the answers to the questions as to When was the earlier transit results by Saturn? How was it? When will it recur? How will it be? can be known from the table below which is for 60 years.

Rasi/Sign	From	To	From	To
Aries	17.06.1968	28.04.1971	17.04.1998	07.06.2000
Taurus	28.04.1971	10.06.1973	07.06.2000	23.07.2002
Gemini	10.06.1973	23.07.1975	23.07.2002	06.09.2004
Cancer	23.07.1975	07.09.1977	06.09.2004	01.11.2006
Leo	07.09.1977	04.11.1979	01.11.2006	10.09.2009
Virgo	04.11.1979	06.10.1982	10.09.2009	05.12.2012
Libra	06.10.1982	21.12.1984	05.12.2012	03.11.2014
Scorpio	21.12.1984	17.12.1987	03.11.2014	27.10.2017
Sagittarius	17.12.1987	20.03.1990	27.10.2017	24.01.2020
Capricorn	20.03.1990	05.03.1993	24.01.2020	17.01.2023
Aquarius	05.03.1993	02.06.1995	17.01.2023	29.03.2025
Pisces	02.06.1995	17.04.1998	29.03.2025	03.06.2027

33.

DATES OF RAHU'S ENTRY INTO A RASI/SIGN

In the below-given Table, the date of entry of Rahu in a Sign is given. Both the nodes Rahu and Ketu always move backwards. If there are any planets in the Rasi/Sign where Rahu enter, kindly know their transit results by reading the early portions of this book. To know the answers to the questions as to When was the earlier transit results by Rahu? How was it? When will it recur? How will it be? can be known from the table below which is for 36 years. As both Rahu and Ketu move simultaneously, their transit results will be concurrent.

Rasi/Sign	From	To	From	To
Pisces	18.08.1986	07.03.1988	25.03.2005	12.10.2006
Aquarius	07.03.1988	24.09.1989	12.10.2006	30.04.2008
Capricorn	24.09.1989	31.04.1991	30.04.2008	17.11.2009
Sagittarius	31.04.1991	30.10.1992	17.11.2009	06.06.2011
Scorpio	30.10.1992	19.05.1994	06.06.2011	24.12.2012
Libra	19.05.1994	06.12.1995	24.12.2012	13.07.2014
Virgo	06.12.1995	24.06.1997	13.07.2014	30.01.2016
Leo	24.06.1997	11.01.1999	30.01.2016	18.08.2017
Cancer	11.01.1999	31.07.2000	18.08.2017	07.03.2019
Gemini	31.07.2000	17.02.2002	07.03.2019	23.09.2020
Taurus	17.02.2002	06.09.2003	23.09.2020	12.04.2022
Aries	06.09.2003	25.03.2005	12.04.2022	30.10.2023

34.

DATES OF KETU'S ENTRY INTO A RASI/SIGN

In the below-given Table, the date of entry of Ketu in a Sign is given. Both the nodes Rahu and Ketu always move backwards. If there are any planets in the Rasi/Sign where Ketu enter, kindly know their transit results by reading the early portions of this book. To know the answers to the questions as to When was the earlier transit results by Ketu? How was it? When will it recur? How will it be? can be known from the table below which is for 36 years. As both Rahu and Ketu move simultaneously, their transit results will be concurrent.

Rasi/Sign	From	To	From	To
Pisces	06.12.1995	24.06.1997	13.07.2014	30.01.2016
Aquarius	24.06.1997	11.01.1999	30.01.2016	18.08.2017
Capricorn	11.01.1999	31.07.2000	18.08.2017	07.03.2019
Sagittarius	31.07.2000	17.02.2002	07.03.2019	23.09.2020
Scorpio	17.02.2002	06.09.2003	23.09.2020	12.04.2022
Libra	06.09.2003	25.03.2005	12.04.2022	30.10.2023
Virgo	25.03.2005	12.10.2006	30.10.2023	19.05.2025
Leo	12.10.2006	30.04.2008	19.05.2025	06.12.2026
Cancer	30.04.2008	17.11.2009	06.12.2026	24.06.2028
Gemini	17.11.2009	06.06.2011	24.06.2028	11.01.2030
Taurus	06.06.2011	24.12.2012	11.01.2030	31.07.2031
Aries	24.12.2012	13.07.2014	31.07.2031	16.02.2033

BACK COVER

Transit of planets is not an unknown concept to the general public as the phrases like 'Sade-Sati' 'Saturn's Dhaiyya' or 'Arthashtama Shani', ' Ashtama Shani' based on Shani's transit and 'Jenma Guru' with respect to Brihaspathi or Jupiter is known even to common people. These are some terms people fear about even though they do not know the intricacies of astrology.

All the planets have their significations and characteristics exhibited by their occupation of a house, associating with other planets, or by their aspect on other planets. Planetary conjunctions, combinations, associations, and aspect present during birth take radical changes during transit and Maha Dasha (Dasha), Antar Dasha (Bukthi), and Prityantar Dasha (Anthram) of planets impact the native's life.

This book deals with the transit of planets over the natal (birth) planets in-depth and beyond comparison. The importance of integrating the planetary combinations with the bhavas and Rasis/signs during transit has been divulged by the author by giving elaborate example charts

The author has given a simple but most important rule as to the **'zero impact'** of transiting planets when they find **no planets** in the house of transit. This rule gives a soothing relief and removes the fear about Saturn and the fiery nodes Rahu/Ketu in the minds of the general public.

The title of the book aptly conveys what is inside in real terms.